Seeking to Understand the World

Literary Journalism of Vincent Sheean

Anish Dave
Georgia Southwestern State University

Series in Literary Studies

Copyright © 2024 Vernon Press, an imprint of Vernon Art and Science Inc, on behalf of the author.

All rights reserved. No part of this publication may be reproduced, stored in a retrieval system, or transmitted in any form or by any means, electronic, mechanical, photocopying, recording, or otherwise, without the prior permission of Vernon Art and Science Inc.
www.vernonpress.com

In the Americas:
Vernon Press
1000 N West Street, Suite 1200,
Wilmington, Delaware 19801
United States

In the rest of the world:
Vernon Press
C/Sancti Espiritu 17,
Malaga, 29006
Spain

Series in Literary Studies

Library of Congress Control Number: 2023936062

ISBN: 978-1-64889-895-2

Also available: 978-1-64889-663-7 [Hardback]; 978-1-64889-689-7 [PDF, E-Book]

Product and company names mentioned in this work are the trademarks of their respective owners. While every care has been taken in preparing this work, neither the authors nor Vernon Art and Science Inc. may be held responsible for any loss or damage caused or alleged to be caused directly or indirectly by the information contained in it.

Every effort has been made to trace all copyright holders, but if any have been inadvertently overlooked the publisher will be pleased to include any necessary credits in any subsequent reprint or edition.

Cover design by Vernon Press. Cover image: Wisconsin Historical Society, WHI-152656. Background image (back cover) designed by aopsan / Freepik.

For my daughter, Tara

Fig. 0.1: Vincent Sheean, *Vanity Fair*, January 1, 1934, Portrait

Contributor: Ben Pinchot/Condé Nast/Shutterstock

The nonfiction writer's goal is to enlarge our understanding of the world.
– Sonja Merljak Zdovc,
"Željko Kozinc, the Subversive Reporter: Literary Journalism in Slovenia," *Literary Journalism across the Globe: Journalistic Traditions and Transnational Influences* (Eds. John S. Bak and Bill Reynolds)

Stories emphasize travel, foreign languages, a sense of looking outward, and a struggle to understand the human condition.
– John S. Bak,
"Introduction," *Literary Journalism across the Globe: Journalistic Traditions and Transnational Influences* (Eds. John S. Bak and Bill Reynolds)

Table of Contents

List of Tables and Illustrations — xi

Foreword — xiii
Douglas Unger
University of Nevada, Las Vegas

Preface — xvii

Acknowledgment — xix

Chapter 1	**Introduction**	1
Chapter 2	**The Making of the Seeker and His Craft**	35
Chapter 3	**Journalism, Writing, and a Passion for People**	59
Chapter 4	**Traces of a Time**	77
Chapter 5	**A Personal Homage to Gandhi**	87
Chapter 6	**In Defense of a Practical Idealist**	97
Chapter 7	**Conclusion**	103

Appendix 1: Select Books by Vincent Sheean — 111

Appendix 2: Archival Sources for Vincent Sheean — 113

Appendix 3: Two Pages from Sheean's Journal, January 21, 1948 — 115

Appendix 4: Two Pages from Sheean's Journal, January 30 and February 6, 1948 — 119

Appendix 5: Sheean's Letter to Ruth Falkenau, a Lifelong Friend, 1927 — 123

Works Cited — 127

Index — 135

List of Tables and Illustrations

Tables

Table 2.1:	A Story Structure of the First Rif Journey Based on Jack Hart's Story Framework	46
Table 2.2:	Two Story Structures of the Second Rif Journey Based on Jack Hart's Story Framework	48
Table 2.3:	The Story Structure of Rayna Prohme's Last Days Based on Jack Hart's Story Framework	52

Illustrations

Fig. 0.1:	Vincent Sheean, *Vanity Fair*, January 1, 1934, Portrait	v
Fig. A3.1.a:	Two pages from Sheean's journal, January 21, 1948	115
Fig. A3.1.b:	Two pages from Sheean's journal, January 21, 1948	117
Fig. A4.1a:	Two pages from Sheean's journal, January 30 and February 6, 1948	120
Fig. A4.1.b:	Two pages from Sheean's journal, January 30 and February 6, 1948	121
Fig. A5.1.a:	A three-page letter by Sheean to a lifelong friend, Ruth Falkenau	123
Fig. A5.1.b:	A three-page letter by Sheean to a lifelong friend, Ruth Falkenau	124
Fig. A5.1c:	A three-page letter by Sheean to a lifelong friend, Ruth Falkenau	125

Foreword

Douglas Unger
University of Nevada, Las Vegas

In order to keep literature alive and thriving, one of the projects of any new generation of scholars must be to study the past for omissions and exclusions from literary history. Books and writers are often overlooked or forgotten. Those deemed relevant or topical for a present era should be reassessed, possibly leading to resurrections of interest and new inclusions in a cannon. Renewed interest in Vincent Sheean and the origins of the genre he pioneered–memoir journalism–which opened up possibilities for "immersion journalism", "saturation reporting" and "new journalism" that followed later is long overdue. Writer-scholar Anish Dave in this study of Vincent Sheean presents a strong case for a thoughtful reassessment of Sheean and his career, with a focus on how his major works of the early to mid-20th century conform to and in some ways helped to invent what literary scholars and teachers now define as established conventions of journalistic writing.

Using close reading and structural analysis, Dave presents Sheean's writing within theoretical genre paradigms established by scholars Jack Hart, Kendall Haven, Marie-Laure Ryan and others. He contextualizes Sheean's best-selling, breakthrough work, *Personal History* (1935), alongside John Reed's *Ten Days That Shook The World* (1919), which preceded it and John Hersey's *Hiroshima* (1946) that followed; both became models for succeeding generations of writers. Sheean's memoir was published with comparable impact and relevance. Dave appraises Sheean also through citing recent studies by scholars Nancy F. Cott, Deborah Cohen, John Maxwell Hamilton, as well as selected commentaries on journalism as a form and what it does best by later 20th century and contemporary writers Tom Wolfe, Ted Conover, Vivian Gornick, and others. Considered within an overview of the history of literary journalism, the intention of Dave's scholarship is to establish Vincent Sheean's credentials as a writer worthy of closer study for what his work can teach and to justify restoring his place in this history.

As a young foreign correspondent in the 1920s, Vincent Sheean secured a position with *The Chicago Tribune* and joined a youthful wave of soon-to-be-famous writer-journalists in Europe that included John Gunther, Dorothy Thompson, William Shirer, and Eric Sevareid (as well as Ernest Hemingway, Malcolm Cowley, and writers of the so-called "lost generation"). Rules for journalism of that era demanded unflinching objectivity, strictly enforced by the *Tribune's* notoriously demanding editors. Sheean often introduced opinion into his journalism, and he was let go from the *Tribune* for unclear reasons. He turned to freelance assignments, following his personal credo, "my own job in my own way" (Hamilton, John Maxwell, *Columbia Journalism Review*, July-August 2008), contributing to *The Atlantic Monthly*, *Harper's*, *The New Republic*, *Century*, and other noteworthy magazines and newspapers. As the post-Great War world divided along ever more dangerous rifts defined by fascism, communism, monarchy and democracy, soon to explode into renewed cataclysm and war, Sheean would be there, following his instincts to pursue stories. As Dave points out consistently in this study, for Sheean, this meant full immersion as both witness to and participant in stories with an artistic dedication to keep improving his craft. Anish Dave earned his M.F.A. in Creative Writing and Ph.D. in Rhetoric and Professional Communication. He applies his skills to close reading of the narrative techniques in Sheean's books, like a jeweler taking apart clocks. *Seeking to Understand the World: Literary Journalism of Vincent Sheean* offers a detailed analysis of Sheean's craft, tracing his methods of achieving story cohesion, dramatic story structures, varying levels of narrator presence, character descriptions, imagery, symbolism, subjective writing, and personal empathy for the people he writes about, all experiments Sheean was trying out that have since become well-established literary nonfiction conventions.

Early in his career, Vincent Sheean made two perilous journeys into a war zone in Morocco to cover the anti-colonialist Riffi rebellion against the Spanish. The Riffi rebels were commanded by Berber leader Abd el-Krim, with whom he secured two exclusive interviews. His first-person account of this dangerous reporting resulted in a work of memoir journalism, *An American Among the Riffi* (1926). This book's modest success propelled Sheean to become more peripatetic as he innovated a style of writing that combined objective reporting, personal story and opinion as he traveled across the globe. He interviewed Spanish dictator Primo de Rivera, covered the rise of Mussolini, the installation of the Shah of Iran, clashes between Zionists and Arabs in Palestine under inept British rule. He wrote about Chiang Kai-shek's early Nationalist victories and his harsh opposition to the Communist wing of the Kuomintang. In China, he met fellow journalist Rayna Prohme. Though she was married, Sheean fell in love, a "love resolved into the largest terms," as Dave cites from a description of their relationship in *Personal History*. Sheean followed her to Russia to cover the 10th anniversary of the Russian Revolution and the founding of the Soviet Union, where Prohme died suddenly, apparently of encephalitis. This personal tragedy moved Sheean to devote his life even more so to pursuing refined language and heightened craft in his writing that defined the literary as he understood it, building on his uses of descriptions, dialogue, and scene-building techniques more expected of novels.

Foreword xv

His breakthrough work, *Personal History* (1935), narrates his travels, stories, and informed judgments of world events with a tragic love story at its heart. It launched as a best-seller and won the inaugural National Book Award for biography. The book would be the source for the screenplay adaptation and movie "Foreign Correspondent" directed by Alfred Hitchcock (1940). Among the many accolades for *Personal History*, Dave cites praise by 1930s literary luminaries Malcolm Cowley and Mary McCarthy, and for its "remarkable achievement in synthesis." As Dave suggests, this synthesis shows Sheean to be a pioneer in what Vivian Gornick describes as "the merger between narrator and subject" (cited from Gornick's seminal text for teachers of literary nonfiction, *The Situation and The Story: The Art of Personal Narrative*). One key to the success of this merger is to maintain a strong focus on the subject as more important than the first-person narrator to avoid solipsism. Sheean's successful exploration of memoir journalism established a new genre for his generation. Dave cites *Saturday Review of Literature* founder and co-editor Henry Seidel Canby on the impact, "a dozen other ex-correspondents have followed his lead," and news reporter Kenneth Stewart, Sheean's contemporary, "Vincent Sheean awakened us as newspapermen to the long view." Books influenced by *Personal History* or modeled after it began appearing, including *On My Own*, by Mary Knight, *Inside Europe* by John Gunther, and *Berlin Diaries* by William Shirer, among a wave of many others.

Vincent Sheean would write and publish at least 27 books, a body of work that spans varying forms of the journalistic memoir, biography, and novels, plus 3 book-length literary translations along with hundreds of articles, news reports, interviews, and commentaries. As a foreign correspondent, he reported on the Spanish Civil War, accompanying Ernest Hemingway and photographer Robert Capa to observe the last gasps of the tragic republican fight against fascism. He was there for Hitler's annexation of Austria and correctly judged the folly of the Munich agreement, then stood by on the banks of the Thames as Nazi bombers devastated London. His books warned the world of the dangers of fascism, and he took strong criticism for suggesting closer foreign policy accommodations with the Soviet Union. During the 1930s and 40s, Sheean seemed to arrive just in time as important stories happened, following an uncanny sixth sense about when, where, and how he could immerse himself and bear witness.

Guided by a close-reading model suggested by Barbara Lounsberry's *The Art of Fact: Contemporary Artists of Nonfiction*, Anish Dave selects from Sheean's body of work five books he deems important for their contributions to memoir-journalism's capacity for expressing topical information, fact-based commentary, and personal experiences that provide readers informed windows into stories. These five works are analyzed for what they reveal and teach us about Sheean's writing techniques and creative process: *Personal History* (1935), *Not Peace but a Sword* (1939), *Between the Thunder and the Sun* (1943), *Lead, Kindly Light* (1949), and *Nehru: The Years of Power* (1960). The story of how Sheean came to write *Lead, Kindly Light* is the most uncanny for his urgent premonition, announced to several acquaintances that he felt certain Mahatma Gandhi would be assassinated. Dave states: "The book, Sheean's personal homage to Gandhi, contains an outstanding story involving Sheean's conversations with Mahatma Gandhi two days before his assassination, which Sheean witnessed…" Dave goes on to describe how Sheean's reaction to this historic event and loss, followed by his traveling on the train carrying the Mahatma's ashes to the holy rivers of Allahabad presents its readers with a transformative, symbolic experience meant to convey the essence of Gandhi's parting message calling for unity, peace, and kindness for the world.

Vincent Sheean's homage to Gandhi, *Lead, Kindly Light*, is his only work available in print at the time of this writing, which feels like a glaring omission from literary history. Since most of Sheean's major works are in the public domain, it seems high time that a university press or an archive press should begin a long overdue process of selected reprints or, at the very least, republications in new digital editions. Whether or not that worthy project happens for the sake of preserving history, Anish Dave's *Seeking to Understand the World: Literary Journalism of Vincent Sheean* makes its own significant contribution to the ongoing life and relevance of Sheean's books for a new generation of readers, scholars, and students of creative writing and journalism. This study should remind us also what it means to write news of the world through a lived experience that seeks to discover and express our common humanity.

Douglas Unger is the author of four novels, including *Leaving the Land*, a finalist for the Pulitzer, and *Voices from Silence*, as well as *Looking for War and Other Stories*. His fifth novel, *Dream City*, will be published in 2024. He is co-founder of the Creative Writing International program at UNLV, where he teaches. He also serves on the Executive Board of Words Without Borders, the nonprofit organization and web publication for world literature in translation.

Preface

In this book, I analyze five journalistic, nonfiction books by Vincent Sheean, an American foreign reporter who was prominent from the late 1930s to 1950s. These books are *Personal History* (1935), *Not Peace but a Sword* (1939), *Between the Thunder and the Sun* (1943), *Lead, Kindly Light* (1949), and *Nehru: The Years of Power* (1960). Vincent Sheean was an important practitioner of literary journalism, as I show in this book. His comprehensive books using literary techniques and crafted writing, along with professional and perceptive journalism, make him a noteworthy author for scholars and students of literary journalism.

My interest in Vincent Sheean was sparked about two years ago when I chanced upon his chapter—from his *Lead, Kindly Light*—on Mahatma Gandhi's assassination. Shortly thereafter, I saw a call for books on literary studies by Vernon Press. A category in the call, literary journalism, caught my attention and I immediately remembered Sheean's chapter. As I read more about Vincent Sheean and literary journalism, it seemed to me that they belonged together. Journalism has always interested me, and I have always found it to be one of the most important professions. Literary journalism combined journalism with writing, my academic discipline.

This book is intended for students and scholars of journalism and nonfiction. They will gain from it an appreciation of how the form of literary journalism was practiced by an able journalist called Vincent Sheean, and why their association was significant for the profession of journalism.

The book's larger role lies in showing why the genre of literary journalism deserves greater attention from scholars of journalism and nonfiction. Literary journalism, such as Sheean's, enhances our understanding of the world, which is so crucial in our technology-immersed times.

Acknowledgment

First, I would like to thank Vernon Press, especially Blanca Caro Duran, Argiris Legatos, and Ellisa Anslow. Without Vernon Press and its excellent team this book may never have been written or published. Their responsiveness, empathy, and kindness kept me motivated and helped me in writing this book. I want to thank the reviewers of the book for their insightful and constructive comments and suggestions.

I want to thank my colleagues at Georgia Southwestern State University, especially from my department of English and Modern Languages, especially Dr. Paul Dahlgren, Dr. Jesse Russell, and Ms. Blue Argo. Their kind words have meant a lot. I'm grateful to the staff of the James E. Carter Library at Georgia Southwestern State University, especially John Wilson, Reference Librarian, for his encouragement, and Adrian Hollomon, Library Technician and Inter Library Loan Assistant, who helped get for me many books on literary journalism that are crucial to this book.

I want to thank Professor Douglas Unger, novelist, my first writing mentor, and the co-founder of the Creative Writing program at UNLV, for his encouragement of this project and for promising any help I needed.

Many thanks to Lee Grady, Reference Archivist, and Lisa Marine, Image Reproduction and Licensing Manager, of Wisconsin Historical Society for their help with the scans of pages from Vincent Sheean's journals and his passport pictures. Thanks also to Jordan Wright, Reader Services and Administrative Assistant, and Catherine Uecker, Head of Research and Instruction, the Hanna Holborn Gray Special Collections Research Center, the University of Chicago Library, for the scans of some of Vincent Sheean's letters. I also want to thank Chris Marino, Research Services Manager, Hoover Institution Library & Archives, Stanford University, for the scans of two of Vincent Sheean's letters.

I'm grateful to Professor John C. Hartsock, a prominent scholar of literary journalism, for his kind response to an important question I had while revising the manuscript of this book. His reply not only answered my question but also motivated me to work harder on the book.

I want to thank my wife, Meeta, for her patient cooperation with my book writing. She has also listened to my occasional monologues while writing and rewriting. Thanks are also due to my friend and colleague Dr. Aditya Simha; my cousin Alka; my brother, Anshuman; his wife, Kanan; and my father, Mukund Shankar Dave; for their encouragement. Finally, I silently thank so many others who, through their words and acts, have helped me grow as a person, scholar, and writer.

Chapter 1
Introduction

Literary journalism seeks a place in both journalism and literature (Maguire and Dow; Kallan). More specifically, it applies techniques of fiction writing to the craft and trade of journalism (Connery *A Sourcebook*). But literary journalism is a "contested" form or genre (Boynton xx; Maguire and Dow 4). Scholars have debated its characteristics and boundaries for a long time, but these debates have been inconclusive. Ben Yagoda aptly describes the form as "profoundly fuzzy" (13). Norman Sims, a reputed scholar of the form, simply notes, "Such definitions are always vague. However well done, they don't necessarily help us distinguish one thing from another" ("Preface" ix).

In his 2007 book *True Stories: A Century of Literary Journalism*, Sims is no more certain: "The nature of literary journalism has evolved during the past several decades, and, at best, definitions have always been a bit vague" (6). Continuing in this vein of scholarly frustration, in a 2015 essay titled "Literary Journalism: Journalism Aspiring to be Literature," journalism professor Miles Maguire admits that "even proponents and practitioners of literary journalism struggle to find the right words to describe it and differ over whether to classify it as a style or an approach to writing or a philosophy of writing and reporting" (362-363). However, Roberta Maguire and William Dow, scholars of English, wisely suggest, "Instead of obsessing with genre issues or scrambling for more taxonomic features…it can be more helpful to see how the modes of literature and journalism fuse and function in individual works produced at specific historical moments and from particular contexts" (4). This book heeds Maguire and Dow's advice and call.

In this chapter, I first review previous scholarship exploring this form, which has attracted several surrogate names. My review is limited to the scholarship on the form involving works of American, and, in a few cases, British journalists and writers. As literary journalism scholars John S. Bak and Bill Reynolds show in their book, however, literary journalism is a global phenomenon. Whether it is interconnections between literature and journalism in Spain (Parratt) or literary journalism helping "political subversion" in Slovenia (Zdovc 254), the form has varied histories and complexities (Bak and Reynolds). Nonetheless, my limited review here does not include scholarship on global literary journalism. Second, I briefly describe my analytical approach or method.

Third, I turn to two renowned American literary journalists who worked as foreign reporters: John Reed and John Hersey. I do this as a prelude—a snapshot of ways in which literary journalism enhances our understanding of foreign lands, peoples, cultures, and events—to the subject of this book: literary journalism of Vincent Sheean, a pioneering and exemplary American foreign correspondent. In addition, my analyses of these two foreign reporters' works of literary journalism also show how this form produces artistic reporting, one that enhances our knowledge of the world by stirring our imagination.

Literary journalism is an especially suitable form for foreign correspondents because it provides deep understanding and arouses our interest and sympathy. As a paragraph on the website of a former, now discontinued, award (Lettre Ulysses) for "literary reportage" states (Hartsock, *Literary Journalism* 85), "Life as a world citizen, on a planet with diverse interdependencies of increasing complexity, demands much more. This world requires many competencies of people: to integrate diversity, to comprehend heterogeneity, to reconcile different layers of information, to interpret context, and to appreciate historical background" ("The Art of Reportage").

In his remarkable career as a journalist and a writer, Vincent Sheean exhibited many, if not most, of these qualities. I end this chapter with a short sketch of Sheean's life and a brief outline of the book. In the chapters that follow, I analyze five of Sheean's nonfiction, journalistic books to show his literary journalism.

Literary Journalism: A Creative, Holistic Genre

In this section, I will first present definitions and characteristics of this form posited by its prominent, mostly American, scholars. I will also list several surrogate names for the genre. Finally, I will summarize a brief history of the genre as traced by Hartsock and a few other noted exponents of the form.

Definitions, Characteristics, and Surrogate Names

Journalism scholar Thomas B. Connery defines literary journalism as "nonfiction printed prose whose verifiable content is shaped and transformed into a story or sketch by use of narrative and rhetorical techniques generally associated with fiction" ("Preface" xiv). Edd Applegate, also representing journalism, defines this form as "writing that combines the literary devices of fiction with the journalistic techniques of nonfiction" (xi). Robert S. Boynton, author and professor of literary journalism, states, "I prefer a functional definition: Acts of literary journalism occur when one explores the factual world in an imaginative manner, the goal being to redescribe and comment on it in story form" (xx). Norman Sims suggests reading works of literary journalism to understand this type of prose: "Reading examples of literary journalism, however, can give one a better sense of the form than definitions can" (*True Stories* xx). Several scholars and practitioners of literary journalism have sought to define the form (or the genre) by describing its features.

In his anthology on New Journalism (another term for literary journalism, as we will see), Tom Wolfe, a prominent practitioner of the genre, lists four principal characteristics of the form:

> scene-by-scene construction, telling the story by moving from scene to scene and resorting as little as possible to sheer historical narrative....dialogue....the so-called 'third-person point of view,' the technique of presenting every scene to the reader through the eyes of a particular character....everyday gestures, habits, manners, customs, styles of furniture, clothing, decoration, styles of traveling, eating...and other symbolic details. (31-32)

In thinking about Wolfe's details about people in the quote (the fourth characteristic), one may consider concrete details in general, often found in descriptions. It may be helpful to get a bit more clarity about the concept of a "scene." According to Sue Hertz, a scholar of English, scenes involve action, speech, and characters (117). Scenes are often discrete units in a narrative, moving it forward but standing on their own (Baldick 323). This construct is also conceived more expansively, as a sort of miniature story (Haven 199). Stories are sometimes distinguished from narratives as involving "characters," their problems, and their "goals" (Haven 11). These concepts will be revisited throughout this book, but it is good to think about them more clearly at this stage.

According to Norman Sims, literary journalism "requires immersion, structure, voice, and accuracy. Along with these terms, a sense of responsibility to their [literary journalists'] subjects and a search for the underlying meaning" ("The Literary Journalists" 8). He explains these features as follows: "Literary journalism demands immersion in complex, difficult subjects. The voice of the writer surfaces to show readers that an author is at work. Authority shows through" (3). Structure "gives order, balance, and unity to a work, the element of form that relates the parts to each other and to the whole" (14).

In a 1995 collection he co-edited with Mark Kramer, Sims quotes Richard Todd, a magazine editor, on the importance of voice in literary journalism: "Voice and story are the only tools" (*Literary Journalism* 9).

On accuracy, Sims states, simply, that "a mandate for accuracy pervades literary journalism" ("The Literary Journalists" 15). On "a sense of responsibility" to subjects (8), Sims recounts interview responses of several literary journalists about a careful balancing act involved in reporting information given by subjects (18-21). Finally, Sims offers the term "symbolic realities" in relation to "a search for the underlying meaning" (22). Probing the term further, Sims bifurcates it into "the inner meaning" (for the writer) and "the deep structures… that lie behind the content" (22).

Barbara Lounsberry, a scholar of English, who terms the genre "literary or artistic nonfiction" (*The Art of Fact* xiii), finds four features in the form: "documentable subject matter chosen from the real world," "exhaustive research," "the scene," and "fine writing" (xiii-xv). She disagrees with Tom Wolfe that dialogue is an essential feature of the genre (xv). Giving an example of John Hersey's *Hiroshima* (which I will analyze in the next section), a seminal work of literary journalism, Lounsberry points out that the book has "little direct quotation" (xv). She ascribes this to a belief that "the scrupulous Hersey did not trust words recollected six months after the atomic explosion" (xv). Furthermore, Lounsberry states that while scenes are important in showing a literary journalist's "artistry," it is good writing that elevates the form to a level where it may be seen and termed as literary (xv).

John C. Hartsock, a scholar of journalism, attributes the following characteristics to the form: "concreteness of description," "the complexity of a portrait," "dialogue," "extended conversation," and "scene setting" (*A History* 28-29). Hartsock emphasizes bringing readers closer to a subject—or subjects—rendered in a work of literary journalism, avoiding "sensationalism" (149).

Ben Yagoda, a scholar of English and journalism, categorizes the pieces included in his co-edited literary journalism anthology as follows: writing that is like "narrative fiction" (alternatively, writing like a "script" from someone "on the scene"), writing by "a reporter at the forefront," and writing with "style as substance" (15-16). While writing that reads like fiction or a script requires a journalist to either "re-create" or accurately relay (15), a reporter immersed in a story "lay[s] bare his or her prejudices, anxieties, or thought processes… [and] gives us something firmer and truer to hold on to as we come to our conclusions" (16). Yagoda mentions four characteristics of the form: "factual"; based on "a process of active fact-gathering"; "currency" (timeliness); and "thoughtfully, artfully, and valuably innovative" (13-14).

In a co-edited anthology, literary journalist Gay Talese and Barbara Lounsberry add a few more features associated with works of literary journalism: "simultaneous narration," "sequential narration," "substitutionary narration," "interior monologue," "imagery & symbolism," "allusion," and "humor" (*Writing Creative* v).

Simultaneous narration is "*narrating consecutively what different individuals are doing* at the same moment in time" (Lounsberry, *Writing Creative* 83, emphasis in the quoted text). Lounsberry has given the example of John Hersey's *Hiroshima* for this type of narration. Sequential narration denotes "*overlapping but* forward moving *sequences of action*" (94). In substitutionary

Introduction

narration, "*the author narrates the story* in the accents and diction of the work's characters" (101). Internal monologue "*is the reporting of a person's internal (often unspoken) thoughts and feelings*" (106). One can narrate in this way only after spending a good amount of time with a subject (106-107). Imagery and symbolism "*bring depth and subtle resonances to a story*" (122). Allusion refers to a range of topics and issues that "*might enrich the context by providing deeper insight into the subject at hand*" (135). Humor "*is a special way of perceiving and presenting the world*" (161).

A few additional points about narratives may be helpful in thinking about literary journalism. In his history of the form, Hartsock insists that the form mainly uses the narrative mode (*A History* 55), but the genre can also include the "discursive" mode (137). In fact, his preferred term for the form is "narrative literary journalism" (87). In a later book, Hartsock defines "narrative literary journalism in part as a genre that emphasizes a personally inflected cultural revelation by means of largely narrative and descriptive modalities" (*Literary Journalism* 83).

In an essay titled "Stories in Essays, Essays as Stories," Douglas Hesse, a scholar of English, argues that stories should be seen as including narration as well as "exposition" (183). Giving examples of George Orwell's "Shooting an Elephant" and E. B. White's "The Age of Dust," both pieces often seen as essays, Hesse asserts that exposition in these "essays" is part of stories—that the essays should be read as stories, which comprise events and the authors' responses to those events (184, 188).

John Warnock, a scholar of English, makes a similar point: "Literary nonfiction may include essay or exposition, but it tends to place these in the context of a story" (xix). Sonja Merljak Zdovc, a Slovenian literary journalist, uses the words "narrative techniques" for writing literary journalism (254). Hesse describes narratives as a "mode" and stories as a "form" (181).

As briefly signaled earlier, the form of literary journalism has attracted several surrogate names. Hartsock lists "literary nonfiction, essay-fiction, nonfiction novel, New Journalism, art-journalism, and journalistic nonfiction," among others (*A History* 4). Connery notes "artistic nonfiction" and "new reportage" ("Discovering" 3). Christopher Wilson records "long-form journalism" and "narrative journalism" ("Chapter 1"). In a later book, Hartsock includes "reportage" (*Literary Journalism* 84), "literary reportage," and "literature of fact" (106).

In summary, I believe that it is useful to think about the genre of literary journalism holistically, by taking a step back if you will: what does it really represent, when it has been defined and described in several ways? The genre appears to be a shape-shifter. In fact, Boynton describes it in precisely these terms: "a protean, fluid genre" (xxi). Maguire and Dow's advice, quoted at the end of the first paragraph in this chapter, seems helpful, if only to discourage what appears to be an illusory goal—striving to define a type of journalism that can take a lot of different shapes, appearances, styles. While it seems reasonable to ponder and discuss strategies or techniques that go into this type of journalism, cutting things too fine to try to pin down the genre seems to be an ineffective pursuit. It is better to accept the genre for what it is, open and broad, and enjoy and analyze works that come close to its general characteristics.

Indeed, John S. Bak, a scholar of American Literature and literary journalism, asserts as much in the introduction of his co-edited book of international literary journalism: "In sum, we have to stop writing definitional manifestos" ("Introduction" 19). He also states that "we should pit international literary journalists against Wolfe's manifesto at times, if only to demonstrate that a European, African, or Asian literary journalism is not like an American literary journalism but that it nonetheless advances our understanding and appreciation of the form" (18). As an example of the variety found in the form, in an essay about literary journalism in Spain in Bak's collection, Sonia Parratt mentions several shapes this genre has taken: "long-form reportages" (139); "creative informative journalism" (141); "nonfiction creative narrative," "long-form, in-depth interpretive stories," "creative journalistic nonfiction narrative" (142); "'noveled' reportage," "literary news writing," "'reportagization' of news" or "'reportaged news'" (143-144); and "biographical reportage" (143).

Another question that can help us think holistically about this genre relates to its significance. Again, Parratt offers a useful insight, stating that "the increase of 'reportaged news' stories in Spanish newspapers today can be traced directly to the need to keep the public's interest—and patronage" (144). If literary journalism generates readers' interest, it is a gain for the profession of journalism and society as a whole. Sonja Merljak Zdovc makes a strong argument for literary journalism, which works perfectly well as an epigraph for this book: "The nonfiction writer's goal is to enlarge our understanding of the world" (242). The following quote about literary journalism is from the "about" page of the website of the Lettre Ulysses Award for the Art of reportage:

> Reportage writers, with their immersion in the subject, bring unknown, hidden or forgotten realities and intricacies to light. By witnessing with their own eyes and collecting and consolidating a mass of information, in forming a picture of the whole, the reportage writer can deliver a greater degree of accuracy than is generally possible with other media formats. This is what gives reportage writing its significance and authority. ("The Art of Reportage")

The quote highlights main strengths of this form or genre: deep, fine-grained, analytical, synthesized, vivid, and, consequently, more accurate journalism.

Another excellent quote that seems to capture an important part of the purpose of this genre comes from Roberta Maguire and William Dow in their introduction to *The Routledge Companion to American Literary Journalism*: "Literary journalism can certainly offer knowledge, but perhaps more legitimately can be credited with fostering modes of public reflection crucial to civil society and social justice" (1). Consider Sonja Merljak Zdovc's description of the writing of Slovenian journalist Zeljko Kozinc: "he could create an image that spoke indirectly about poverty, and this proved effective in influencing his readers' emotions" ("Željko Kozinc, The Subversive" 250). She adds that Kozinc "was able to introduce social and political criticisms of the social system in which people struggled for survival despite the state's claims of social equality" (249-250). Next, I provide a brief historical overview of the genre.

A Brief Historical Overview of Literary Journalism

In his important book tracing the genre's history, John C. Hartsock looks as far back as Plato (*A History* 133) and ancient Rome for the origins of literary journalism. Among the Roman ancestors of the form, according to him, were informational and narrative accounts known as *acta diurna* and *acta populi Romani*, respectively (83-84). More pointedly, he credits the period between the beginning of the sixteenth century and the start of the twentieth century C. E. as one that contributed to the development of the form. He mentions both British and American examples of what he calls were "antecedents to a modern narrative literary journalism" (87) or "early literary journalism" (96). These examples include *Nine Daies Wonder* by William Kemp (1600), *The Wonderfull Yeare* by Thomas Dekker (1603), Mary White Rowlandson's account of "her captivity among Indians" (1682) (109), "Edward 'Ned' Ward's sketches of London life" (1698-1700) (111), Daniel Defoe's *Journal of the Plague Year* (1722), and Henry David Thoreau's "four sketches about Cape Cod" (1855) (129).

Toward the close of the nineteenth century, the objective style of journalism gained ascendancy in the U.S. (Hartsock *A History*). Narrative literary journalism seems to have emerged as a reaction to an objectified news style (Hartsock *A History*). The post-Civil War period until the end of the nineteenth century was a period of important changes and crises in the U.S., and narrative literary journalism was a response to changing times (Hartsock *A History*). Narrative literary journalism was also connected to two contemporary literary movements, literary realism, and naturalism (Hartsock *A History*). Prominent practitioners of narrative literary journalism during this period included Stephen Crane, Lafcadio Hearn, Theodore Dreiser, and Abraham Cahan (Hartsock *A History*). Hartsock distinguishes narrative literary journalism from narrative yellow or sensational journalism and muckraking, two similar journalistic strains during this period (*A History*). The main distinction between the variants, according to

Hartsock, was the ability of narrative literary journalism to narrow the gap between the author of a work and his subject or subjects (*A History* 142). By reducing this gap, the literary journalist empowered readers to participate in imaginatively creating the subject or subjects (Hartsock *A History*).

According to Hartsock, the periods during which "modern narrative literary journalism in the United States" grew were "the 1890s and the first decade of [the twentieth] century; the 1930s and 1940s; and the new journalism of the 1960s and 1970s" (*A History* 153). These periods find an agreement with the assessment of Thomas B. Connery (*A Sourcebook*). Some of the literary journalists during the early decades of the twentieth century were John Reed, Ernest Hemingway, John Dos Passos, James Agee, and Joseph Mitchell, among others (Sims "Preface"; Applegate).

A special mention must be made of New Journalism, a phenomenon of literary journalism which flourished "from the mid-1960s to the mid-1970s" (Sims, "The Literary Journalists" 6). Most literary journalism scholars do not consider New Journalism to be *sui generis* or without precedent (Hartsock *A History*; Applegate; Sims, "The Literary Journalists"; Arlen). Hartsock posits that the distinguishing quality of this manifestation of literary journalism was "that it achieved considerable critical recognition" (*A History* 191). According to Norman Sims, "The New Journalism era was a breakout decade for literary journalism in the twentieth century" (*True Stories* 23). American Studies scholar Ronald Weber states that "one of the noteworthy features of American writing throughout the 1960s and 1970s has been the prominence of journalistic nonfiction" (*The Literature* 1). Weber explains that the New Journalism of the 1960s arose in a condition in which realistic fiction came to be seen as unrepresentative of prevailing realities in American life (11). New journalism was an attempt to construct the realities better (10-13). Representative writers—journalists—of New Journalism were Tom Wolfe, Truman Capote, Hunter Thompson, Joan Didion, and Norman Mailer (Sims *True Stories*). In his anthology on New Journalism, Tom Wolfe also includes Gay Talese, Jimmy Breslin, Gail Sheehy, Michael Herr, and Joe McGinniss, among others (39).

Two more matters need to be briefly noted before I close this historical overview. One is the international reach of literary journalism. *The International Association for Literary Journalism Studies (IALJS)* was founded in 2006 for "encouragement and improvement of scholarly research and education in literary journalism (or literary reportage)," as stated on the organization's website. Maguire states that "further establishing the study of literary (or narrative) journalism on the larger scholarly agenda was the…founding and subsequent growth of the *International Association for Literary Journalism Studies (IALJS)* and its journal, *Literary Journalism Studies*" ("Literary Journalism: Journalism Aspiring" 362). In addition, as John S. Bak states, "there exists a rich

Introduction

international contingent of literary journalism and literary journalism scholars" ("Introduction" 2). In his collection of essays on international literary journalism co-edited with Bill Reynolds can be found an essay on literary journalism in Spain by Sonia Parratt and another on Slovenia by Sonja Merljak Zdovc. Parratt discusses a complex history of literary journalism in Spain, pointing out that the genre is practiced in different forms and enjoys a wide readership. Sonja Merljak Zdovc analyzes the literary journalism of her mentor, Zeljko Kozinc, showing how he deepened readers' understanding of his society while being mindful of his country's communist politicians.

The second matter concerns contemporary literary journalists. A few of them mentioned by literary journalism scholars are Ted Conover, Tracy Kidder, Michael Paterniti, Susan Orlean, William Langewiesche, Aman Sethi, among many others (Sims *True Stories*; Rajan; "The Art of Reportage"; Harrington and Sager). Next, I will explain the method I used to write this book.

Method

I use close reading or analysis (also called textual analysis) as a method. Catherine Belsey, a scholar of English, defines textual analysis or close reading "as a research method involv[ing] a close encounter with the work itself, an examination of the details without bringing to them more presuppositions than we can help" (160). She adds that "the way to use secondary sources is very sparingly indeed. I prefer to make a list of the questions posed by the text and arrive at my own tentative, provisional answers, and only then to read other people's interpretations" (164). Close reading, according to Belsey, is thus immersing oneself in a text, no doubt aided by note-taking, highlighting, and supplementary reading to better understand textual information and issues. Belsey also implies that for her the text is preeminent. It both answers to issues raised by the text and guides her research further. I followed Belsey's approach as I worked on this book.

I closely read five nonfiction, journalistic books by Vincent Sheean, an American foreign correspondent (see Sheean's biographical sketch later in the chapter). These books include *Personal History* (1935). *Not Peace but a Sword* (1939), *Between the Thunder and the Sun* (1943), *Lead, Kindly Light* (1949), and *Nehru: The Years of Power* (1960). I selected his nonfiction, journalistic books for foreign reporting because Sheean was a foreign reporter. He wrote many other books as well. In the following chapters, I analyze each of these books for their features of literary journalism.

I also closely read John Reed's *Ten Days That Shook the World* and John Hersey's *Hiroshima* for my analyses of these books, presented in the next section.

I chose Vincent Sheean's books to evaluate him as a literary journalist because "Mr. Sheean's effort was best fulfilled in his books, to which he devoted most of his career after 1925" (Montgomery). Throughout his career, Sheean also wrote news stories and articles. However, he wrote many books, including fiction, and several were based on his journalistic work (I have chosen five of these for my analysis). It is important to note that "many of the best-known works of narrative literary journalism are now read in book form" (Underwood 272). Notably, too, several literary journalism scholars have analyzed this genre or form in books written by the form's recognized practitioners (Lounsberry *The Art of Fact*; Weber *The Literature*).

Scholars of literary journalism have frequently used close reading as a method to analyze works of literary journalists. Thomas Connery points out that "in exploring new journalism or literary nonfiction, Hollowell and Weber rely on close readings of texts" ("Discovering" 22). In his *Fact & Fiction: The New Journalism and the Nonfiction Novel*, John Hollowell, a scholar of English, states, "I have selected works by Truman Capote, Norman Mailer, and Tom Wolfe for close analysis" (x). Differentiating between reading and analysis, Hollowell adds that "the short view [textual analysis] permits the close reading of particular texts" (xi). Ronald Weber describes his method as follows: "I want...to see how particular examples of literary nonfiction work, how they are put together and what their effects are; I want, in other words, to talk about the work as it is, in all its variety and complexity" (*The Literature* 3). Weber's quote aptly describes my own approach to the analysis of Sheean's books; I too focused on books by Sheean I analyzed and only supplementarily on brief reviews of his books or on biographical material about him. Connery informs us that "Lounsberry turns to her five writers to demonstrate the artistry of their nonfiction through close readings" ("Discovering" 25). He further notes that "Lounsberry provides a comprehensive...exploration of their nonfiction."

Based on her analysis of John McPhee's select works, Lounsberry asserts, "McPhee strives always for the fullest, 'panoptic' vision. Thus his works, characteristically, include not only natural description, but also the historical, scientific and technical, religious, sociological, biographical (and even autobiographical) dimensions that contribute to each scene" (*The Art of Fact* 106). Similarly, Lounsberry analyzes Didion's "first three works of literary nonfiction—*Slouching Towards Bethlehem* (1968), *The White Album* (1979), and *Salvador* (1983)" (109). Describing her method in the book, Lounsberry writes, "Because so little has been attempted, the chapters that follow, largely formalist in cast, seek to offer strong readings of the works of Talese, Wolfe, McPhee, Didion, and Mailer—perhaps the five most prominent contemporary artists of nonfiction" (xvi).

Introduction

Similarly, Daniel Lehman, a scholar of English, examines works of literary journalism by John Reed, an American reporter, using close reading or analysis (*John Reed*). A more recent example of close reading to analyze works of literary journalism can be found in Journalism scholar Richard Lance Keeble's co-edited volume on international literary journalism (*Global Literary*). Describing the analytical method of his co-editor, John Tulloch, who contributed a chapter in the book, Keeble writes, "Examining closely the intros (first paragraphs in newspaper jargon) of 12 of [Geoffrey] Moorhouse's journalistic books and articles...Tulloch suggests...they are 'artful constructions with a precise visual reference, a conjoining of observed "fact" with the imaginative exploration of a state of mind'" (*Global Literary* 12).

Although close reading is also called close or textual analysis, scholars need to read a text before they can analyze it at length. I followed close reading of Sheean's books with an analysis focusing on their literary journalism characteristics. My review of literary journalism scholarship was key to my analysis. In addition, I used concepts and frameworks from books on narratives and stories, mainly *Story Craft: The Complete Guide to Writing Narrative Nonfiction* by Jack Hart, *Write Right! Creative Writing Using Storytelling Techniques* by Kendall Haven, and Marie-Laure Ryan's article "Narrative" in *Routledge Encyclopedia of Narrative History* edited by David Herman, Manfred Jahn, and Marie-Laure Ryan.

I also read a few contemporaneous reviews of Sheean's books. Finally, I read a few biographical sources about Vincent Sheean, either fully or in part. These mainly included Carl Edward Johnson's 1974 doctoral thesis about Vincent Sheean titled *A Twentieth Century Seeker: A Biography of James Vincent Sheean*, Nancy F. Cott's *Fighting Words: The Bold American Journalists Who Brought the World Home Between the Wars*, Deborah Cohen's *Last Call at the Hotel Imperial: The Reporters Who Took on a World at War*, John Maxwell Hamilton's essay titled "Vincent Sheean's *Personal History*" in *Second Read: Writers Look Back at Classic Works of Reportage* edited by James Marcus and the *Columbia Journalism Review* staff, and a chapter in John Maxwell Hamilton's *Journalism's Roving Eye: A History of American Foreign Reporting* (chapter 13 "My Own Job in My Own Way").

Finally, I want to add that, like any analysis, my analysis of Vincent Sheean's nonfiction, journalistic books should be seen as one way to understand these works for their literary journalism qualities. Other scholars interested in Vincent Sheean can find other ways of analyzing his voluminous books.

I now turn to the analysis of two stellar works of literary journalism by two American foreign reporters, John Reed, and John Hersey. These two journalists and their two works briefly analyzed here are better known to many literary journalism scholars than Vincent Sheean and his journalistic works. I will discuss a few likely reasons for Sheean's relative obscurity among scholars of literary journalism in the concluding chapter of this book. Here it is important to reiterate that I wish to examine these two well-known works before delving into Sheean's books because doing so may help us see the suitability of this form for foreign reporters. Additionally, the two books by Reed and Hersey analyzed here show why literary journalism is an artistic form. Works in this form not only improve one's knowledge of events but encourage multiple perspectives and empathy, benefits that are valuable in our understanding of international affairs. Both the works came out of their writers' immersion in the settings for the works, another quality of literary journalism.

Two American Foreign Reporters and Their Iconic Works

Literary journalism scholars have noted several American writers of this form who worked as foreign reporters or correspondents. Some of those mentioned in the scholarly literature are Mark Twain (Connery *A Sourcebook*; Applegate), Julian Ralph (Applegate), John Reed (Wolfe; Connery *A Sourcebook*; Sims and Kramer; Lehman *Matters*; Sims *True Stories*; Bak "Of Troops"; Roberts), Ernest Hemingway (Kerrane and Yagoda), A. J. Liebling (Sims "The Literary Journalists"; Bak "Of Troops"), John Hersey (Wolfe; Flippen; Hollowell; Connery *A Sourcebook*; Kerrane and Yagoda; Sims *True Stories*; Kramer "Coming"; Bak "Of Troops"), Martha Gellhorn (Sims *True Stories*; Kerrane and Yagoda), Ernie Pyle (Connery *A Sourcebook*; Bak "Of Troops"), Vincent Sheean (Applegate; Weber *The Literature*; Arlen), Mary McCarthy (Sims and Kramer), and Michael Herr (Wolfe; Kerrane and Yagoda).

In this section, I analyze John Reed's *Ten Days That Shook the World*, originally published in 1919 (Chutchian 37). The book describes the happenings during the Russian Revolution of November (based on the New Style calendar, as Reed informs us in his book) 1917, when the Bolsheviks seized power. Before my analysis of the book, I provide a summary of Reed's biography. Next, I analyze John Hersey's *Hiroshima*, which was first published in *The New Yorker* in 1946. *Hiroshima* is narrated through stories of six survivors of the atomic bomb attack on Hiroshima, Japan, on August 6, 1945. Hersey added a fifth and final chapter to the book in 1985. As with Reed, before my analysis of Hersey's work, I provide background information about John Hersey.

I chose these two works for my analysis because they have been widely acclaimed by scholars of literary journalism. A quick look at the number of citations after the names of Reed and Hersey in the first paragraph of this section hints at the popularity of these two journalists among literary journalism scholars. Their two works that I analyze here are often mentioned as outstanding examples of literary journalism. Reed's work has also found some criticism, which I will briefly discuss. Applegate calls *Ten Days That Shook the World* "an example of literary journalism" (212) and "probably Reed's greatest achievement because it accurately informed readers about a major event." About Hersey's *Hiroshima*, John S. Bak notes, "Yet it is for *Hiroshima* (1946), which New York University lists as the greatest piece of American journalism of the twentieth century, that he is most recognized" ("Of Troops" 246). The second reason for my choosing these two journalists was that they both worked as foreign correspondents for at least some time. In other words, they were not simply foreign reporters for an occasional journalistic mission or assignment.

John Reed

John Reed was born in Portland, Oregon, on October 22, 1887, to C.J. Reed, a business executive, and Margaret Green, daughter of a local businessman (Rosenstone 9-13). After completing his schooling, Reed entered Harvard University (38). He published fiction and verse in the *Harvard Monthly* (39). He also participated in activities of a drama club and a club in which American and international students mingled (44-46). At Harvard, a composition teacher named Charles Townsend Copeland inspired Reed to pursue "adventure and heroism in the modern world" (47). Reed wrote for a humorous Harvard publication called *Lampoon*, "where he poked fun at professors, students, radicals, clubs, football, suffragettes, marriage, the *Crimson*, Boston society— and himself" (54). At the end of his college career, Reed was an action-oriented young man who "thought himself...a writer" (57).

Lincoln Steffens, a newspaper editor at the close of the nineteenth century, who wanted his reporters to be literary (Connery "A Third Way" and *A Sourcebook*), got Reed his first job in journalism at *The American Magazine* in 1911 (Rosenstone 77-78). In 1912, Reed joined the editorial board of a socialist-leaning publication called *The Masses*, which was edited by Max Eastman (107-109). In 1913, John Reed found a cause that appealed to his nature (119, 397). He went to Paterson, New Jersey, to find out about striking silk workers in the town (119). While he observed the strikers, the local police arrested him (120). After his release, he wrote a "hard-hitting, vivid, and angry" article for *The Masses* (123).

In late 1913, Reed became a foreign reporter for the *Metropolitan* magazine. He was tasked with reporting on a revolution in Mexico (150-153). Biographer Robert Rosenstone writes that "Reed also obtained an assignment from the New York *World* to supplement his income" (151). From his work in Mexico came several articles for *Metropolitan* and pieces for *The Masses* (Lehman, *John Reed* 97). Daniel Lehman, who has analyzed Reed's works of literary journalism, writes that Reed's "front-page exclusive interviews with Pancho Villa and Venustiano Carranza [leaders of the Mexican revolution] appeared in the *World* on March 1 and 4, 1914—pieces that cemented Reed's reputation as a foreign correspondent" (97). Later, Reed used material from his reporting to publish a book, *Insurgent Mexico* (96). Although Lehman criticizes Reed for taking liberties with factual details in the book (based on Lehman's research involving Reed's notes), he acknowledges that "Reed manages a significant break in *Insurgent Mexico* from the ruling notion of how to cover alien culture" (94). According to Lehman, in his work, Reed showed "evidence" of "the ethical implications of reproducing human life and death" (94-95).

In 1914, Reed went to Europe to cover the war for *Metropolitan* (Lehman 144). Lehman praises Reed's reporting on the war as one that was "more ready to see it in a larger political context" (147), adding that "Reed takes every opportunity to explore the horrific impact of war on both French and German soldiers" (147-148). In 1915, Reed also reported for *Metropolitan* from "the Balkans and Russia" (155). Reed went to Russia before the Russian Revolution in November (according to the New Style calendar) 1917, carrying press credentials from the New York *Call* and *The Masses* (174). Reed's magnum opus, "the book that built Reed's lasting reputation" (172), *Ten Days That Shook the World*, was written based on his experiences during this visit. Although Reed was widely criticized for sympathizing with a communist revolution (Chutchian 106-108; Lehman 196), the book acquired an "enduring power" (Chutchian 120). It "was praised by U.S. diplomat and Russian expert George Kennan several decades later" (120). John Reed died from typhus in Russia in 1920 (Applegate).

In addition to *Ten Days That Shook the World*, Applegate mentions Reed's *Insurgent Mexico* as another example of literary journalism. Both books were products of foreign reporting.

Ten Days...: Like "a Movie Script"

Ten Days That Shook the World describes the November 1917 Russian Revolution, based on the new style of calendar. Although the Bolsheviks captured power on November 7, the forces impelling the revolution had been afoot for days and even months before (Reed). Regarding the dates in the book, John Reed himself writes, "I have adopted in this book our calendar throughout, instead of the former Russian calendar, which was thirteen days earlier" (Reed 27).

In the literary journalism anthology edited by Kevin Kerrane and Ben Yagoda, Yagoda classifies their selections according to three categories. The first category of "narrative journalism," according to Yagoda, has "two substrains," one based on a novel and the other based on a "movie or play" (15). Explaining the second kind, Yagoda writes, "The reporter is on the scene and more or less matter-of-factly relates what happens, in the manner of a script." He further explains that "much of the artistry here lies in the reporter's retreat from our vision, whether as partial or full-scale 'fly on the wall.'" Yagoda's subcategory of a report that is scripted like a movie or play seems to aptly describe John Reed's *Ten Days That Shook the World*. The book is considered a "masterpiece" of literary journalism (Bak, "Of Troops" 240), though a few scholars have raised a few critical questions (Hartsock *Literary Journalism*).

For example, John Hartsock agrees with historian A. J. P. Taylor, who wrote an introduction to the Penguin edition of the book, that "Reed's book founded a legend, one which has largely triumphed over the facts" (*Literary Journalism* 115). However, other literary journalism scholars disagree with Hartsock and Taylor (see Applegate; Lehman *John Reed*). Lehman mentions "Reed's Russian notebooks and the boxes of handbills, speeches, pamphlets, and newspapers he carried back with him from Petrograd" (*John Reed* 184). Albert Rhys Williams, a fellow American reporter who was with Reed in Petrograd during the time of the revolution, describes Reed's reporting during those days and calls *Ten Days*... "unmatched" (125). Somewhat inexplicably, Taylor, too, notes earlier in his introduction that "the book is not only the best account of the Bolshevik revolution, it comes near to being the best account of any revolution" ("Introduction" vii). Reed himself portrays his book in this way: "This book is a slice of intensified history – history as I saw it....a chronicle of those events which I myself observed and experienced, and those supported by reliable evidence" (*Ten Days* 9). Reed includes information in the book about his "sources" in a concise way (27-28). At the start of his comments about the sources, he states, simply, that "much of the material in this book is from my own notes" (27).

Yagoda's conception of a piece of narrative journalism that is like a film appears to find support in Reed's own words explaining his rationale for the book: "Just as historians search the records for the minutest details of the story of the Paris Commune, so they will want to know what happened in Petrograd in November 1917, *the spirit which animated the people, and how the leaders looked, talked, and acted* [emphasis added]. It is with this in view that I have written this book" (Reed, *Ten Days* 13). According to the *Concise Oxford American Dictionary*, the verb "animate" means "bring to life" ("Concise" 30). *Roget's International Thesaurus* lists "motion-picture" as one of the synonymous categories of words for the word "animated" ("Animated" 527). In this category, one further finds words such as "cinema," "cinematic," "filmistic," "filmic," and so on. Thus Reed's words "the spirit which animated the people" have cinematic connotations. Similarly, Reed's words "how the leaders looked, talked, and acted" remind one of films, in which actors do these very things. In the analysis below, I further show how the book creates an effect of a film.

Reed begins with two chapters giving contextual information to readers. In the first of these chapters, he explains Russian terms for the country's social and political institutions. Although this chapter is full of contemporary Russian terms, concepts, and names, the information is not overwhelming because Reed has divided the chapter into headings and sub-headings, making the task of reading easier. In the second chapter, titled "Background," Reed narrates and describes the state of the country at the time of the revolution—a divided people, class-consciousness, growing popularity of the Bolsheviks, economic inequality and hardships, corruption, among other things. Having thus prepared the reader to follow him into the revolution, almost as though one watched a short exposition at the start of a historical film, Reed follows a more-or-less chronological structure (despite occasional backtracking in the narration), describing the revolution through its main stages.

Film scholar Vincent LoBrutto explains a typical structure of a film as follows:

> The great majority of films of the twentieth and twenty-first centuries are built on a three-act structure. In the first act the narrative situation is established and the characters are introduced. It ends with an event that propels the story into the second act. The second act deals with that event and also deals with whatever other minor storylines have been established in the first act. The third act is the resolution and completion of the story. (240-241)

Reed's book seems to reflect this structure. The first three chapters, along with the preface, serve as the first act, setting the context for the narrative of the revolution to follow. As has been partly stated, in these chapters, Reed provides information about Russia's social and political entities, the happenings in the country, and the dissimilar political forces. It is not until the third chapter, "On the Eve," that we encounter what may be called precipitating events that impel us into the second act: the overthrow of Russia's provisional government headed by Kerensky (Reed, *Ten Days* 97). Chapters 4 through 10, "The fall of the Provisional Government," "Plunging Ahead," "The Committee for Salvation," "The Revolutionary Front," "Counter-Revolution," "Victory," and "Moscow," respectively, constitute the second act of the narrative (88, 117, 145, 164, 181, 200, 219). In these chapters, readers see the main events of the revolution: the attack on Winter Palace in Petrograd, the seat of Russia's provisional government; Kerensky's flight; battles between the fighters of the revolution and those defending the old order; and the triumph of the Bolsheviks. The chapters contain scenes, actors, dialogue, texts (speeches, decrees, and the like), and detailed description—aspects of literary journalism. The third act concludes the success of the Bolsheviks and their gaining the support of peasants.

Introduction

The book is crammed with details: movements and gatherings of people; meetings; speeches; resolutions; orders; newspaper reports; actors of all kinds and persuasions, working together, opposing one another, following, leading; conflict; to name a few things. Such lifelike details (Kramer, "Breakable Rules" 23), which are central to literary journalism, lend a quality to Reed's book resembling a film, imparting an "immediacy" to a narrative, a "gripping or absorbing quality" (Wolfe 31).

Another filmic technique Reed uses is known as "sectional analytical montage" (Zettl 315). This narrative technique "temporarily arrests the progression of an event and examines an isolated moment from several viewpoints. It shows the various sections of an event and explores the complexity of a particular moment." Reed uses this type of narration at a number of places in the book. For example, in the chapter titled "On the Eve" (*Ten Days* 63), Reed describes various actions by dissimilar actors at or around the same time. The day is November 3, 1917. Reed "waited in the corridor" outside a "meeting of [Bolshevik leaders] behind closed doors" (73). One "Volodarsky...came out [and] told [him] what was going on." Reed tells us that "Lenin spoke." After describing the gist of Lenin's comments (based on what Volodarsky told him), Reed turns his attention to an "upstairs room" in which "sat a...certain Avseenko, called Antonov...drawing careful plans for the seizure of the capital." Then, Reed informs us what the government was doing: "The *yunker* artillery was drawn into the Winter Palace. Patrols of Cossacks made their appearance in the streets for the first time since the July days." Finally, Reed mentions an editorial comment by "Novoye Vremya (New Times)," a "bourgeois" newspaper, decrying the government for "no...authority" (73-74). Through a wide survey of different moves, Reed shows us the magnitude and complexity of the revolution at a particular juncture.

Vivid descriptions add to the book's cinematic quality and literariness. These descriptions provide what Wolfe calls "symbolic details...of people's status life" (32). A description helps us see the leaders of the revolution:

> Before the door of Smolny was an automobile. A slight man with thick glasses magnifying his red-rimmed eyes, his speech a painful effort, stood leaning against a mud-guard with his hands in the pockets of a shabby raglan. A great bearded sailor, with the clear eyes of youth, prowled restlessly about, absently toying with an enormous blue-steel revolver, which never left his hand. These were Antonov and Dybenko. (Reed, *Ten Days* 171)

Another portrait shows a scene inside Winter Palace on November 7, 1917, as seen—and imagined—by John Reed:

> The long table covered with green baize was just as they had left it, under arrest. Before each empty seat was pen, ink, and paper; the papers were scribbled over with beginnings of plans of action, rough drafts of proclamations and manifestos. Most of these were scratched out, as their futility became evident, and the rest of the sheet covered with absent-minded geometrical designs, as the writers sat despondently listening while Minister after Minister proposed chimerical schemes. I took one of these scribbled pages, in the handwriting of Konovalov, which read, "The Provisional Government appeals to all classes to support the Provisional Government – " (110-111)

In the passage, Reed is partly speculating about—or imagining—the way the members of the provisional government who sat around the table deliberated before they were forced to end their meeting. Passages like these may have given a reason for Reed's critics (e.g., historian A. J. P. Taylor) to doubt the veracity of some of his assertions in the book. In Reed's defense, however, it can be said that he gives several concrete details in the passage that may help one draw a more complete picture. One more example of a description is worth giving because it provides a glance and an echo of the revolution caught by Reed while on a train to a nearby suburb in hopes perhaps to learn about the battle between the revolutionaries and their opponents:

> Through the window we could see, in the swiftly deepening darkness, masses of soldiers going along the muddy road towards the city, flinging out their arms in argument. A freight-train, swarming with troops and lit up by huge bonfires, was halted on a siding. That was all. Back along the flat horizon the glow of the city's lights faded down the night. A streetcar crawled distantly along a far-flung suburb…. (173)

Literary journalism scholars consider scenes to be a distinguishing mark of this form (Wolfe; Connery *A Sourcebook*). Two memorable scenes in Reed's book are his entering, along with a few others, into Winter Palace on the day when the provisional government falls; and a scene in which Reed is forced "down from the truck" (Reed, *Ten Days* 213) in which he is riding together with revolutionary soldiers. A critical moment in this scene comes when Reed realizes that the soldiers who ordered him off the truck because they could not understand his official pass were thinking of killing him. Reed manages to steer them in the direction of a distant house in hopes that someone there may explain his pass to his captors. Reed is proved right and set free. Both scenes are novelistic, full of dialogue.

Immersion or, in the words of Wolfe, "saturation reporting" (52) is another well-known characteristic of literary journalism. Reed's immersion can be sensed from the following paragraph by Albert Rhys Williams, another American journalist who was already in Petrograd when Reed "arrived by train from Stockholm" (Williams 21).

> Together Reed and I discussed the course of the Revolution to date, especially as we crossed the Liteiny or the other bridges from Petrograd and entered another world—the slums, the tenements, the cramped, crowded settlements of the workers around the huge armament plants and smoky mills. Reed, sniffing the air, surveyed the air and said, "I thought this was 'feudal Russia.' Smells more like Pittsburgh to me. You talk to these Mensheviks and Social Revolutionaries and you get the idea that capitalism hasn't touched Russia. How come?" (26)

It is such insights, synthesized and subjective, based on immersion in a setting, that gives literary journalism its power.

Finally, one last point about Reed's lack of neutrality in writing his book must be noted because it has invited criticism of literary journalism scholars (Hartsock *Literary Journalism*; Roberts). Reed writes in his book that he did not claim neutrality, but that he tried to report like "a conscientious reporter" (*Ten Days* 13). Hartsock calls Reed's work "the monologic of a history" (115). A biographer of Reed accuses him of having "blinders on" (Chutchian 119). It is indeed true that Reed's work sees Bolsheviks in a sympathetic light. However, he does not entirely shun the other side or point of view, as a quick look at the table of contents in Ten Days . . . may show. Two chapters have titles representing anti-Bolshevik forces: "The Committee for Salvation" (Reed, *Ten Days* 145), made up of Russian politicians opposed to Bolsheviks, and "Counter-Revolution" (181). Lehman refers to these chapters in rejecting the notion that Reed's work was "a single-voiced celebration of Soviet victory" (*John Reed* 180). Indeed, throughout Reed's book can be found newspaper reports both supporting and opposing Bolsheviks' position. For example, at one of the meetings after the collapse of Russia's provisional government, Reed records how one Avilov, speaking on behalf of parties opposed to Bolsheviks, receives "some clapping" after his "cool, tolerant reasoning" (140-141). At another meeting, Reed notes, "Now a Bolshevik was speaking, one of their own men, violently, full of hate. They liked him no more than the other [a reference to the previous speaker, probably "a Menshevik," opposed to Bolsheviks]" (155). Thus, taking into account evidence from *Ten Days* . . . in totality, Reed's account appears to be a detailed but a sympathetic account of the November 1917 Russian Revolution.

John Hersey

John Hersey was born to missionary parents, Roscoe and Grace, on June 17, 1914, in Tientsin (now Tianjin), China (Treglown x, 20; Hersey, "Homecoming-I" 49). His father joined the Tientsin mission of the Y.M.C.A. in 1905 (Hersey, "Homecoming-II" 46). Herseys returned to the U.S. in 1925 due to Roscoe Hersey's health problems (Hersey, "Homecoming-I" 49). Recalling an early global influence, John Hersey writes that "the Tientsin of my boyhood was a polyglot town" (65). In his biography of Hersey, Jeremy Treglown observes that "in retrospect it was the cosmopolitanism that struck him most: the distinctiveness of each foreign quarter of Tientsin" (9).

After attending Hotchkiss, "an elite boarding establishment," on a scholarship, John Hersey attended Yale University (Treglown 25). Treglown tells us that "in articles for the university paper he had…been learning to be a writer" (32). Later, "Hersey joined the editorial board of the Yale Daily News—the oldest college daily paper in the United States" (32). In this matter, we can see a similarity between John Hersey and John Reed, who also wrote for his college newspaper. Hersey's "own interests were soon reflected in the paper" (32). For example, the newspaper published his "front-page interview with an American Asia expert, George Sokolosky, about the recent collision between the League of Nations and Japan over the latter's incursions into Manchuria" (32).

After Yale, Hersey "went to Clare College, Cambridge, on a Mellon scholarship" (Treglown 33). In 1937, Hersey left his studies at Cambridge to become a personal assistant to famous American novelist Sinclair Lewis (38-39). Then, Hersey joined *Time* magazine and was assigned to the "foreign news section," tasked with covering Japan and China (45). Later, he became one of the magazine's "associate editors" involved in "putting together the Foreign News section" (50). Treglown writes that in addition to editing foreign reporting, Hersey prepared "cover stories" for the magazine, an article on Churchill, a piece on Greece, and so on (60). Soon after, Hersey became a *Time-Life* war correspondent for the Pacific (69). He also published books based on his experiences covering the war: *Men on Bataan*, "a book on the battle of the Philippines and Douglas MacArthur" (64), and *Into the Valley*, based on the American offensive in Guadalcanal (71-72). In 1945, Hersey won the Pulitzer Prize for Fiction for his novel *A Bell for Adano* (Treglown 86), a story based on "the Allied occupation of Italy" (Michaud).

In 1944, Hersey went to Moscow, Russia, as *Time-Life*'s foreign correspondent (Treglown 93-94). In 1945, Hersey left his job at *Time-Life* (108). Hersey found a new publication in *The New Yorker*, for which he contributed a number of pieces from China, while also writing in *Life* (111-114). It was for *The New Yorker* that Hersey wrote "Hiroshima," which the magazine carried in its August 31,

1946 issue. A 1993 obituary of the writer published by the magazine called "Hiroshima" arguably "the most famous magazine article ever published" ("John Hersey" 111). Alfred A Knopf published it as a book, which "sold some three and a half million copies, in many editions, and is still in print" ("John Hersey" 111). In all, Hersey published in *The New Yorker* "some two dozen...nonfiction pieces...over a period of forty-four years" ("John Hersey" 111). John Hersey passed away due to cancer on March 24, 1993 (Treglown 287).

In addition to *Hiroshima*, which is "considered one of the central works of the genre [of literary journalism]" (Jones 213), another notable literary journalistic work of Hersey that is set abroad is *Into the Valley* (Applegate). Hersey accompanied the soldiers on the operation that the book describes (Treglown 72).

Hiroshima: Compact and Profound

Hiroshima narrates and describes the experiences of six survivors of the August 1945 atomic bomb attack on Hiroshima, Japan. The book is divided into four chapters, and a fifth chapter—an epilogue—was added by Hersey nearly forty years after the book's publication. The first chapter, "A Noiseless Flash" (Hersey 3), describes the moment the bomb was dropped on Hiroshima and the subsequent minutes and hours. The second chapter looks at the immediate impact of the bomb. The third chapter gives a more drawn-out account of the bomb's effects, including rescue efforts. The fourth and the final chapter of the original work provides an even longer, a more extended view of the bomb's consequences, especially for the six survivors. The fifth chapter that Hersey added in 1985 completes the stories of the six survivors, answering the question of what happened to them in later years.

In his anthology on New Journalism, Tom Wolfe calls *Hiroshima* "very novelistic" (46), acknowledging its "influence" on writers such as Truman Capote, a fellow New Journalist. Wolfe prefaces his remark by stating that in Hersey's book "we start getting into the direct ancestry of the present-day New Journalism." Indeed, *Hiroshima* follows Wolfe's criteria for New Journalism quite well, as may be judged by his rather unreserved praise for the work (which in any case is almost universally praised). In addition, a number of other characteristics for literary journalism proposed by other scholars can also be seen in the book. Let's begin with Wolfe's criteria. They are, briefly, "scene-by-scene construction," dialogue, the "'third-person point of view,'" and "symbolic details...of people's *status life*" (Wolfe 31-32).

In chapter two, titled "The Fire" (Hersey 25), there is a gripping scene involving one Mr. Fukai, an official at the Catholic mission whose German pastor, Father Wilhelm Kleinsorge, is one of the six survivors. As Father Kleinsorge is preparing to leave "the mission compound" (15), amid fires everywhere, someone draws his attention to Mr. Fukai "standing in his window on the second floor of the mission house" (37). Father Kleinsorge manages to reach Mr. Fukai and, despite his inexplicable demands to be left alone, gets him out of the building. Father Kleinsorge then carries Mr. Fukai piggyback to reach a safe area. However, once when the pastor loses his footing, Mr. Fukai finds an opportunity to escape and takes off in the direction of the danger. Kleinsorge asks some nearby soldiers to block the running man, but Mr. Fukai eludes them. This compelling scene gives way to another scene, involving another pastor, Mr. Tanimoto.

Mr. Tanimoto, another member of the six survivors, is running to his church and is also looking "for his family" (Hersey 39). He sees fires and destruction all around along with horrific suffering of the victims. Although he tries to help on occasion, he is not successful. At last, he finds himself swimming in a river, trying to get to the other shore. Once there, he miraculously finds his wife and "their infant daughter" (41). After a brief exchange with his wife, he resumes his trudge toward his church and reaches an area where Father Kleinsorge has sought refuge. Mr. Tanimoto asks the German priest about Mr. Fukai, and Father Kleinsorge tells him that Mr. Fukai "ran back" (43). This scene involving Mr. Tanimoto is followed without interruption by another scene focusing on Miss Sasaki, yet another survivor. Miss Sasaki works in a factory and has been trapped inside her office after the explosion. She is finally freed, but "her left leg" is "badly broken and cut" (44). In addition, she finds herself accompanied by two badly "wounded people."

In this way, scene by scene, chapter two moves forward. According to author and journalism scholar Jack Hart, "you use each scene to frame the action, gripping your audience in the developing drama" (88). In terms of "action" and "developing drama," the second chapter has scenes that amount to what R. Thomas Berner calls "showing" as opposed to "summary" (*Writing Literary* 5). Chapter one involves "simultaneous narration" or "narrating consecutively what different individuals are doing at the same moment in time" (Lounsberry, *Writing Creative* 83). Narration drives the whole book, recounting the lives of the six survivors of the atomic bomb blast, with occasional explanation.

Wolfe's second criterion of dialogue finds only limited application in *Hiroshima*. Lounsberry convincingly argues that "this is probably because the scrupulous Hersey did not trust words recollected six months after the atomic explosion" (*The Art of Fact* xv).

Wolfe describes his third criterion of a "third-person point of view" as "presenting every scene to the reader through the eyes of a particular character" (32). As shown above, chapter two uses a shifting point of view, seeing the immediate effects of the explosion through the eyes and minds of Mr. Tanimoto, Mrs. Nakamura, Father Kleinsorge, Dr. Fujii, Dr. Sasaki, and Miss

Introduction

Sasaki. Indeed, the "third-person point of view," as Wolfe defines it, is present throughout the book.

Finally, "symbolic details...of people's *status life*" ("everyday gestures," "habits," "customs," along with a host of other distinctive aspects of people) (Wolfe 32) fill the book. To Wolfe's conception, we may add concrete details in general. Some sundry examples of such specifics in the book include "cross-legged" sitting of Dr. Masakazu Fujii, one of the six survivors, at the start of the book; Father Kleinsorge's "reading a Jesuit magazine, *Stimmen der Zeit*" (Hersey 3); Mr. Tanimoto's facial features; "moxibustions," "the ancient Japanese treatment" (101); names of local newspapers; "Japanese custom" (13); physical features of Father Kleinsorge; names of places in and around Hiroshima; names of rivers in the city; names of bridges; Japanese words; injuries sustained by the bomb victims; signs of destruction in the city; people's names; Dr. Sasaki's writing of his patients' records in German (94); and radiation symptoms.

Two other points should suffice to conclude this analysis of *Hiroshima*. The first is a characteristic of literary journalism that Lounsberry terms "fine writing" (*The Art of Fact* xv). She mentions a few qualities of such writing—"assonance and alliteration," "parallel structures and repetitions," "metaphors," and "plain prose"—but the phrase can be used to describe other markers of distinguished writing. Indeed, in a later book, Lounsberry adds scenes, types of narration, "imagery & symbolism," "allusion," and "humor" as ways to write in a literary style, emphasizing that these ways "do not exhaust all the possibilities" (*Writing Creative* v, 77). Another point I need to make before concluding this analysis relates to "symbolic realities," a characteristic of literary journalism according to Norman Sims ("The Literary Journalists" 22).

Differentiating between structure and style in writing, Lounsberry states that "the narrative form and structure disclose the writer's artistry; and...its polished language [style] reveals that the goal all along has been literature" (*The Art of Fact* xv). Although Lounsberry appears to equate her phrase "fine writing" somewhat restrictively with the writing style, I conceive of the phrase as including both structure and style. In the following analysis, I illustrate this point. Structure and style are intertwined in Hersey's book.

Despite the fact that *Hiroshima* is narrated from six different points of view, in addition to the author's own point of view present in explanations or "historical narration" (Wolfe 31), the book displays a remarkable "global coherence," a unity as a work (Williams and Bizup 113). If not for this quality, the book may have been seen as a fragmented narrative, comprising varied accounts of six survivors of the atomic bombing. I suggest that there are four strategies that help achieve this global coherence: 1) the chronological structure (Williams and Bizup) of the book; 2) evocative chapter titles, similar to what Williams and Bizup call "forecasting themes" (114); 3) the "opening segment" of the book (Williams and Bizup 117); and 4) writing that carefully balances details with conciseness. While the first three strategies relate to the structure of the book, the last strategy relates to its writing style.

The book follows a chronological structure, beginning at the time the bomb is dropped and following its aftermath through hours, days, months, and years. According to Joseph Williams and Joseph Bizup, both scholars of English, this structure is the "simplest order" (118). It is easy to follow and understand. This structure also provides a global coherence to the work because the structure presents stories involving a specified period, which begins with the explosion and ends, by chapter four, about a year from the attack, and, by chapter five, at a historical distance spanning a few decades. Readers finishing the book are likely to find it coherent because of this structure, commonplace to our lives. As Williams and Bizup state, "Coherence is an experience we create for ourselves as we make our own sense out of what we read" (113).

The second strategy of evocative chapter titles is like starting "each new section with a heading that includes the key themes for that section" or starting a section with a brief opening about its content (Williams and Bizup 114). Such titles provide thematic coherence to every chapter. In addition, the chapter titles of "A Noiseless Flash" (Hersey 3), "The Fire" (25), "Details are being Investigated" (57), "Panic Grass and Feverfew" (89), and "The Aftermath" (121) show a chronological progression. Together, these chapter titles read as parts of a single and larger story.

The opening segment of the book—the third strategy contributing to the book's global coherence—briefly introduces the six survivors and narrates where they were and what they were doing when the atom bomb exploded in Hiroshima. This short introduction and narrative encompassing the six survivors is followed by a brief summary of this catastrophic event. The opening segment suggests that the book will tell the stories of these six survivors. Thus, the opening segment, comprising 345 words, contributes to the global coherence of the book by informing the reader at the very start what the book will include. This point brings us to the book's writing style, another factor contributing to the book's global coherence. This factor can be summed up as a balancing act between a need for details and a need to be concise.

A careful balancing of conciseness and informativeness helps with a consistent tone in the book. This factor also contributes to the book's global coherence. As Susan Bell explains in her book on editing, a "continuity of tone…holds a text together and helps it move forward," while endowing the text with a certain "atmosphere" (86-87).

Conciseness is perhaps especially worthy in a subject matter so grave. It has the effect of making sentences emphatic, in keeping with the event that the

Introduction

world had never before witnessed (or indeed did not experience afterwards, except at the second bombing on Nagasaki). Writer Pamela Haag notes the effectiveness of "writing about complex things simply, with a cadence and style that are exceptionally clear" (229). She also suggests to "slow down for solemn moments." Both these techniques are on display throughout the book, as can be seen in its limpid sentences. To achieve a balancing act between necessary details and concise prose, the book uses modifiers, semicolons to extend sentences, and parenthetical explanations.

A modifier is a "part of a sentence [that] extends, clarifies, or qualifies another part" (Bacon 77). It can be "a word, a phrase, or a dependent clause" (78). Modifiers can be "initial modifiers," "medial modifiers," or "end modifiers" (79-84). The first sentence of the book contains four initial modifiers and a medial modifier: "At exactly fifteen minutes past eight in the morning, on August 6, 1945, Japanese time, at the moment when the atomic bomb flashed above Hiroshima, Miss Toshiko Sasaki, a clerk in the personnel department of the East Asia Tin Works, had just sat down at her place in the plant office and was turning her head to speak to the girl at the next desk" (Hersey 3). The initial modifiers are phrases starting from "At exactly fifteen minutes…" to "at the moment when…," four in all. The medial modifier is the position description of Miss Sasaki, "embedded within the main clause" (Bacon 79). Modifiers help convey as much information as possible without adding more sentences and tedium to the book.

The book also uses semicolons to extend sentences, thus adding to its compactness. Here is one example involving "structures…placed in apposition," that is, "structures…placed alongside a clause or phrase of the same type, with the same referent" (Bacon 131). Bacon explains that "the second clause or phrase will be read as a modifier restating or elaborating on the first."

> The next things he was conscious of were that he was wandering around in the mission's vegetable garden in his underwear, bleeding slightly from small cuts along his left flank; that all the buildings round about had fallen down except the Jesuits' mission house, which had long before been braced and double-braced by a priest named Gropper, who was terrified of earthquakes; that the day had turned dark; and that Murata-*san*, the housekeeper, was nearby, crying over and over, "*Shu Jesusu, awaremi tamai!* Our Lord Jesus, have pity on us!" (Hersey 17)

The passage uses dependent clauses starting with "that" and placed *in apposition* to present additional information concisely (my emphasis). The information in the sentence given above depicts the experience of Father Kleinsorge, a survivor of the bombing, immediately following the explosion of the bomb.

Additionally, the book uses parenthetical explanations to supplement its narrative. These clarifications provide additional, contextual information briefly, without distracting the reader from the narrative. For example, in the second chapter, Mr. Tanimoto sees that "huge drops of water the size of marbles began to fall...[and] half thought that they must be coming from the hoses of firemen fighting the blazes" (Hersey 26). After this text, there appears in parentheses a clarification of what Mr. Tanimoto saw: "(They were actually drops of condensed moisture falling from the turbulent tower of dust, heat, and fission fragments that had already risen miles into the sky above Hiroshima.)" The parenthetical explanation gives scientific information about the phenomenon that Mr. Tanimoto saw concisely, enclosed inconspicuously in parentheses.

An analyst exploring the book for its "symbolic realities" (Sims, "The Literary Journalists" 22) may find a few directions in the book. Sims interviewed Richard Rhodes, a literary journalist, who informed Sims that he found "deep structures" in his writing about nuclear weapons (22). Rhodes' book *The Making of the Atomic Bomb* was published in 1986. Rhodes told Sims about his accumulated anger from his troubled childhood. The "deep structures" in the book for Rhodes relate to his decision to put his "anger and passion to moral and social use" (the bomb seemed "A symbol of...anger," according to Rhodes) (Sims, "The Literary Journalists" 23). Sims tells us that "symbolic realities" in a work of literary journalism "has two sides": the "meaning" of a work for its writer and the "meaning" that underlie a work itself or its "content" (22).

In *Hiroshima*, evidence for any symbolic realities shaping the book may be seen in chapter five, which was a later addition. Among the clues are news snippets regarding atomic weapons. Here are a few examples: "*On July 1, 1946, before the first anniversary of the bombing, the United States had tested an atomic bomb at the Bikini Atoll.*" (Hersey 175, emphasis in the original text). Another such text reads: "*On September 23, 1949, Moscow Radio announced that the Soviet Union had developed an atomic bomb*" (179, emphasis in the original text). There are five more such news items, set off from the book's narrative. Reading these news items, all of which are in chapter five, in conjunction with the last paragraph of the book, both in its final version and in the original, 1946 version (published in *The New Yorker*) with only four chapters, may offer an insight into the book's larger meaning.

In the 1946 version, the last paragraph of the book calls attention to the effects of the bomb on children: "It would be impossible to say what horrors were embedded in the minds of the children who lived through the day of the bombing in Hiroshima" (Hersey 117-118). The paragraph includes an anecdote involving a ten-year-old boy, Toshio Nakamura, who survived the bombing. He quotes briefly from an essay he wrote describing his experience. In the present version of the book, with five chapters, the last paragraph describes Mr.

Tanimoto in the seventh decade of his life, nearly four decades after the atomic bomb explosion. The paragraph mentions his "snug little house with a radio and two television sets, a washing machine, an electric oven, and a...compact Mazda automobile" (195-196). Mr. Tanimoto "got up at six every morning and took an hour's walk with his woolly dog, Chiko" (196). When we juxtapose the two last paragraphs in both versions of the book and the news snippets about atomic weapons, we see two vastly divergent futures for the world. It can be one in which our children thrive and do not feel threatened, or it can be one that endangers children, in which might is right, and nations compete with one another to amass deadlier weapons. The two final paragraphs also show that despite numerous differences, most people share common concerns and desires (to protect and love children, to enjoy pets, to drive automobiles, to watch television programs, and so on).

The analyses of John Reed's *Ten Days That Shook the World* and John Hersey's *Hiroshima* show that literary journalism is a well-suited form for foreign reporting. Unlike traditional journalistic accounts, literary journalism provides an in-depth account of events and people in foreign countries, enabling a better understanding of people, issues, and potential problems. In a recent article on John Hersey, Roy Scranton, a scholar of English, sums up the value of literary journalism for foreign reporting: "Close attention to the specific details of complex global events is a wedge that can be driven into the seemingly inevitable progression of the past, and might also help us perceive turning points in the present."

Literary journalism also appeals to our imagination and knowledge of the world. Although Reed's account of the Russian Revolution has its critics, it is undeniable that a person who lives a century after the event can see and feel in the account what it might have been like, a sort of time travel via a book. The same thing can be said about Hersey's *Hiroshima*. It is a book that takes one closer to the horrible event, via one's imagination, ideally leaving people more determined to make better choices for the world.

In the next section, I provide a biographical sketch of Vincent Sheean, another foreign correspondent, whose literary journalism is the subject of this book. Applegate includes Vincent Sheean in his anthology of literary journalists, which comprises both writers and editors. Weber mentions Sheean in his 1980 book *The Literature of Fact: Literary Nonfiction in American Writing*. Michael J. Arlen refers to Sheean in a chapter titled "Notes on the New Journalism" (244). More recently, journalism scholar John Maxwell Hamilton argues that Sheean exemplifies "informed reporting of the highest order" ("Vincent Sheean's" 131) and that his *Personal History* [Sheean's memoir, published in 1935] "is still a potential beacon for journalists seeking to recover the purpose and credibility" (125). Hamilton considers Sheean a model to "encourage correspondents to interpret the world for an audience that often doesn't have the background to weigh a leader's quote or judge the relevance of a distant fact" (131). Referring to Sheean's famous 1935 memoir, *Personal History*, Nancy F. Cott, a scholar of American History, writes that it "brought Sheean transatlantic fame. It...won a National Book Award (in the inaugural year of the prize)" (206). Briefly reviewing *Personal History* two years after its publication, Henry Seidel Canby observes that the book "strike[s] deeper than journalism" (4). He adds that "Sheean's job was to get the news, but in getting it, he learned to think what it meant."

Vincent Sheean: A Foreign Reporter and a Writer

James Vincent Sheean, who was known professionally as Vincent Sheean and to colleagues and friends as Jimmy, was born in Pana, Illinois, on December 5, 1899, in a family of Irish immigrants (Johnson, iii, 1-5; Hamilton, "Vincent Sheean's" 124). His father, William Sheean, with whom young James had a difficult relationship, was a "traveling salesman"(Johnson 4). Sheean was close to his mother, Susan, who inculcated in him an early love for literature and reading (Johnson 4-8). In his doctoral thesis, a comprehensive and well-researched biography of Vincent Sheean, Carl Edward Johnson describes other early literary influences on Sheean: a priest who taught him French (19) and an English teacher (14-16).

In 1917, Sheean enrolled at the University of Chicago (Johnson 26; Cott 9). Following his mother's death, he left the university in 1921 without completing the required coursework to obtain a degree (Johnson 46-50). However, Sheean's "language study, begun in Pana and enriched in Chicago (fourteen of the thirty-two courses he took at the university were foreign language courses), adequately prepared him for his life as foreign correspondent" (Johnson 51). Johnson also mentions Sheean's work for the university newspaper (32) and his literary production, which included a play (46). A May 1920 issue of *The University of Chicago Magazine* names Sheean in connection with a play: "The men who are responsible for the modernity of this year's production are James Vincent Sheean, 21, and Harold Stansbury, 20, the authors" (The Alumni Council 256). The magazine goes on to say that "Sheean came to college with a typewriter under each arm. Started right in as a Freshman by working on the Maroon....Since then he has written news for the United Press, United News and the Herald and Examiner."

After leaving the university and a very short employment with the *Chicago Daily News* (Johnson 49), Sheean went to New York, where he joined the *New York Daily News*, covering divorces and other scandals (Applegate; Johnson 61; Cott 15-16). By 1922, Sheean was in Paris, working for the European edition of the *Chicago Tribune* (Cott 24). Shortly thereafter, he was assigned the "foreign

Introduction

desk" (Johnson 74). Sheean's reporting took him to Switzerland, Germany, Italy, Spain, and Morocco (Weber, *News of Paris* 169-170).

Johnson mentions a news story by Sheean in the *Chicago Tribune* on November 26, 1923, about an experiment the newspaper conducted. Sheean led the plan, in northern Rhineland in Germany (85-86). The country had been asking the U.S. for food assistance, and the newspaper had received reports that local farmers refused to sell food against the weak German currency (Sheean, "16 Die in Ruhr" 1). Sheean headed an effort by a group of seven poor Germans moving from farmhouse to farmhouse in search of food. Sheean's account of the episode includes dialogue and vivid description, techniques of literary journalism. In the story, Sheean mentions that "a man shouted he would put the dogs after us if we did not move on" (2). At the next house, Sheean's group received better treatment. But a woman who came to the door refused to sell any produce, protesting that "the big hotels can pay in Dutch and American money." Summing up his newspaper experiment, Sheean states, "Geese were eating cabbages at one place and cows were eating turnips at another, but the people refused to give or sell us food." Sheean effectively portrays an 81-year-old German widow, a grandmother who wanted potatoes for her grandchildren (1-2).

Sheean made two risky and extended excursions into the Rif region of northern Morocco to find out about the struggle by the Riffian people against Spain and, later, France, their colonial masters. He interviewed the rebels' leader (Cott 87-95). Out of his experiences of the first trip, full of adventure, came his first book, *An American Among the Riffi*, published in 1926 (Cott 99). In this book, according to Johnson, "Sheean can be seen as a precursor of the new journalism in his use of fictional techniques in a non-fiction work. His study of the Rif amounted to 'saturation reporting,' with its sharp characterization, narrative detail and skillful dramatic effect" (117).

In 1925, Sheean's job with the Paris edition of the Chicago *Tribune* ended, somewhat anticlimactically, due to a misunderstanding between Sheean and his employers (Hamilton, "Vincent Sheean's" 125-126; Weber, *News of Paris* 170). After some time, Sheean began to write for the *North American Newspaper Alliance* (*N.A.N.A.*) (Johnson 119-120). From this point onward, Sheean remained a freelancer for the most part, securing assignments and credentials from newspapers, magazines, or news organizations (such as *N.A.N.A.*) to cover news stories and pay for expenses (Weber, *News of Paris* 170; Cott, 93, 148). In addition to *N.A.N.A.*, Sheean also worked on a freelance or flexible basis with the New York *Herald Tribune* and the *Paris Times* (Weber, *News of Paris* 170; Johnson 281). Sheean also wrote news articles for magazines such as *Asia* and *Holiday* (Johnson 141, 518; Cott 100, 309).

During the 1920s, in addition to Europe, Sheean visited Persia, China, Russia, and former Palestine, following his keen and intuitive sense for news stories (Cott 200).

In 1935, Sheean's famous memoir *Personal History* came out. The book narrated a decade of Sheean's life, starting at the University of Chicago and moving through his journey as a foreign reporter. It is widely considered to be his best work (Johnson 720-721). Decades later, his obituary in *The New York Times* dated March 17, 1975, mentions *Personal History* as "his best-known book" (Montgomery). In her review of *Personal History* in *The Nation*, novelist Mary McCarthy writes, "His book is only incidentally a chronicle of events; it is, at bottom, a serious study of the relation of an individual to the world. Sheean's clear-sighted perception of this problem, his peculiar, passionate approach to it, turn a lively, well-written piece of journalism into a first-class literary work" (284).

In the next few years, Sheean wrote two more memoirs, the result of his journalistic journeys around the world during the 1930s and early 1940s: *Not Peace but a Sword*, published in 1939, and *Between the Thunder and the Sun*, published in 1943. *Not Peace...* examines events and situations in Europe leading up to the Second World War: London, the Spanish Civil War, the persecution of Jews, and Czechoslovakia. Sheean was on the ground, in London observing people, their culture, their institutions; meeting with American volunteers fighting on behalf of the republican forces in Spain and traveling through the embattled landscape; driving around in Czechoslovakia and witnessing Nazi propaganda; in a whirlwind period of reporting from March 1938 to March 1939 (Sheean, *Not Peace* 364). In his contemporary review of the book, Franz Hoellering, journalist and film critic, describes the book as part of "the genre of his great success—reporting in a literary style that goes beyond newspaper writing. Presenting the temperament, the feelings, and thoughts of the observer as he looks at worlds great and small" (128).

Between the Thunder... covered a longer period compared to *Not Peace...*, roughly from 1935 to 1941, beginning at Cannes in France and moving through Italy, France, England, the United States, and China—to the last via countries in the Pacific and Southeast Asia. Again, Sheean is intensely involved in events and people around him. Reviewing the book in the *New York Times*, Craig Thompson writes, "With Mr. Sheean the generous use of the first person singular does not become oppressive....Instead it becomes the badge of a sensitive reporter trotting a troubled globe....It lends the continuity of autobiographical narrative and the steadiness of a fixed, consistent viewpoint to a collection of scenes, actions and conversations" (4).

A "note" in *Between the Thunder...* informs that at the time of the book's publication, Sheean was a Major in the U.S. Army Air Forces. Sheean joined on

Introduction

May 28, 1942 (Sheean, *Between the Thunder* 421). He was promoted to Lieutenant Colonel in 1943 (Johnson 412). As a serviceman, Sheean worked as an intelligence officer (427). He received his official discharge in October 1944 (426).

In 1946, Vincent Sheean went to Lawrenceburg, Tennessee, to cover a trial of 25 African Americans for an "attempted murder" in a case involving the racial conflict (Johnson 479). An April 1947 issue of *Nieman Reports*—a publication of the Nieman Foundation at Harvard University, which promotes "thought leadership in journalism" (https://niemanreports.org)—republished a news story by Vincent Sheean about the case, titled "Present Day American Tragedy," which had originally appeared in the New York *Herald Tribune* (Sheean, "Present Day" 16-17). The *Nieman Reports* news story carried the following brief note: "The Nieman Fellows of 1945-46 made a blueprint of the kind of newspaper they would like to see. They selected this story from the *New York Herald Tribune* to illustrate what they mean by reporting" (16).

In January 1948, Vincent Sheean traveled to India. He had an astonishing premonition that Mahatma Gandhi, the main leader of India's struggle for freedom, would be assassinated by a fellow Hindu (Sheean, *Lead, Kindly* 176). Johnson mentions that Sheean "did have hunches, premonitions, forebodings and he did acquire the habit of anticipating events and cataclysms. All this would culminate in his journey to India to see Mahatma Gandhi in 1948" (265). Sheean interviewed Gandhi on January 28, 1948, two days before his assassination. Sheean was present in Birla House on January 30, where Gandhi had been living, and saw Gandhi walk out from his room to the garden where he held his prayer meeting. Then, Sheean heard the shots that ended Gandhi's life. In 1949, Sheean published *Lead, Kindly Light*, a book about Gandhi's life and message, with a lengthy appendix discussing elements of Hinduism, Gandhi's approach to questions of faith and religion, and spiritual leaders of India who preceded Gandhi. The book includes Sheean's interviews with Gandhi during his final days, a personal account of Gandhi's assassination, and events of Gandhi's last rites. According to Cott, the book was a tremendous success (313). In his review of the book for the *New York Times*, Louis Fischer describes the chapters containing Sheean's personal reaction to Gandhi's assassination and the rites that followed to be the "best" part of the book ("Light from India" 3, 24).

In 1960, Sheean published another book about India. This time, he wrote a book about Jawaharlal Nehru, a prominent leader of India's struggle for independence, India's first prime minister, and Gandhi's political heir. Louis Fischer also reviewed this book for the *New York Times*. He praises it as "a portrait illuminated by love of his subject" ("Highlights and Shadows" 6), but he also finds the book to be inadequately critical of India's foreign policy stances.

In addition to journalistic, nonfiction books already mentioned, Sheean wrote several news stories and articles, short stories, novels, and biographies (see Johnson, pages 740-754, for a detailed list of Sheean's publications; a select, books-only bibliography is given in Appendix 1). Two of Sheean's more successful novels were *Sanfelice* (1936) and *A Day of Battle* (1938) (Johnson 333). Vincent Sheean wanted to make his mark as a novelist, a goal in which he was somewhat successful, compared to his successful journalistic nonfiction (Johnson 724; Weber, *News of Paris* 170-171).

Walt Harrington, a literary journalism scholar and author, uses the term "personal journalism" to describe journalistic stories or articles written with a dominant "I" or a "personal lens" ("Preface: When Writing" xviii-xxi). Yet Harrington adds a note of caution: "[Such] stories were personal but not self-indulgent or narcissistic. In fact, the journalists writing them were brave souls willing to reveal themselves—often in a strange or sorry light—in order to bring readers insights that were deeper than supposedly objective third-person stories" (xviii). Sheean would certainly agree with this description of the term. Sheean told Carl Edward Johnson, who was working to write Sheean's biography for his doctoral thesis, that "if a writer has given himself [or herself] to his work and is no longer self-seeking, the work often becomes great" (Johnson 719).

Sheean wrote biographies of Mahatma Gandhi (in addition to *Lead, Kindly Light*), Thomas Jefferson, Oscar Hammerstein I, and Edna St. Vincent Millay (Johnson 742). He published articles in venues such as *The Atlantic, New Republic, Foreign Affairs,* and *Virginia Quarterly Review* and short stories in publications such as *Women's Home Companion, Saturday Evening Post,* and *Harper's Magazine* (Johnson 744-754).

Vincent Sheean saw writing as his "raison d'etre" (Johnson 457). He told Johnson that "the great writer goes beyond the good writer in his [or her] respect for the language" (718-719). In a recent book, history scholar Deborah Cohen mentions Sheean's belief in an idea called "One Worldism" (414), a "vision of interdependence" among nations favored by Wendell Willkie, a former U.S. presidential candidate (Zipp 14).

Toward the end of the 1950s, Sheean began to work for Westinghouse Broadcasting Company (Johnson 693-695). In the next decade, he left the U.S. and settled in Arolo, Italy (Johnson 702). Vincent Sheean died on March 15, 1975 (Montgomery).

Lastly, I briefly introduce the remaining chapters.

Brief Chapter Outlines

In chapter two, I analyze Sheean's *Personal History*, published in 1935. I argue that the book's novelistic character is due to the skillful cohesion of its varied narratives. Four factors contribute to the cohesion: a linear, chronological structure; simple and short chapter titles; frequency of stories; and crisp, informative sentences. Additionally, a distinctive narrator's presence also helps with the cohesion.

In chapter three, I examine *Not Peace but a Sword*, which came out in 1939, Sheean's successor journalistic memoir to *Personal History*. This book's case for literary journalism rests on a much-praised story and a few lifelike scenes, the book's spartan language, and the use of vivid details.

Between the Thunder and the Sun, the subject of chapter four, was published in 1943 and is more episodic. Aspects of this journalistic memoir that could be seen as literary journalism include its strong character portrayals, its use of imagery and symbolism, and its subjective writing.

In chapter five, I analyze Sheean's *Lead, Kindly Light*, which appeared in 1949. The book, Sheean's personal homage to Gandhi, contains an outstanding story involving Sheean's conversations with Mahatma Gandhi two days before his assassination, which Sheean witnessed because he had gone to meet with Gandhi that evening. Sheean's reaction to this historic incident and his travel on the train carrying the Mahatma's ashes for their immersion in the holy rivers of Allahabad are also parts of the story in the book. I argue that the story and its symbolism make a convincing case to be seen as literary journalism.

Chapter six briefly examines Sheean's memoir—published in 1960 and titled *Nehru: The Years of Power*—about Jawaharlal Nehru, the first prime minister of India and a leading figure in India's fight for freedom alongside Gandhi. The book's more modest case to be seen as a work of literary journalism depends on the use of an effective symbol, clarity in explaining India's careful foreign policy, and a personal portrayal of Jawaharlal Nehru as a leader.

Finally, in the concluding chapter, I explore a few questions about Sheean's literary journalism: his place—or absence—in the scholarship, his humanism, and his literary journalism in foreign reporting, a useful example to emulate in today's world.

Chapter 2
The Making of the Seeker and His Craft

Toward the end of *Personal History*, which was published in 1935 and won the first National Book Award for Biography (Cott 204; Hamilton, "Vincent Sheean's" 128), its author Vincent Sheean reproduces a conversation he has been having with Rayna Prohme, his communist friend who died in Russia two years before. Sheean tells the reader that his friend did not "appear" to him as if in a vision, but that he still had an exchange with a "force" that could be given her name (*Personal History* 397). Sheean had just returned from what was former Palestine, and the conflict between Jews and Arabs that he witnessed there—"the violence of August 1929…ignited" over the Western Wall (Winder 11)—anguished him. It seems to have made him introspective. As he wondered about his purpose in the vast and complicated world, he heard Rayna Prohme's sage advice about what he should do with his life:

> Your work, if you ever do any that amounts to a damn, will have to be some kind of writing, I suppose; I don't know much about that, but it might be a good idea to try to learn how to write. And if you ever do learn how, the obligation upon you will be just this: to see things as straight as you can and put them into words that won't falsify them. That's programme enough for one life, and if you can ever do it, you'll have acquired the relationship you want between the one life you've got and the many of which it's a part. (Sheean, *Personal History* 396-397)

At first glance, a call "to learn how to write" may seem unusual from a writer who in the next few years would publish this intricate and voluminous book. However, at the time of the events covered in the book, Sheean was in his early writing career. He began writing *Personal History* in 1934 (Johnson 223). In 1926, he published *An American among the Riffi*, an account of his first visit to the Rif region in northern Morocco (Cott 99). Of this early book, Johnson writes that "the account proceeds much like a fictional narrative" (116), but that the book did not show "growth in the writer, only episodic excitement" (117). According to Johnson, before *Personal History*, Sheean's "literary production had hardly lifted him to the status of a 'serious writer'" (223).

Other evidence for the quote's call to learn to write can be found in *Personal History* itself. In the book, Sheean tells the reader about his desire to write well, while admitting that he had not yet become disciplined enough to do so

(*Personal History* 212). Sheean also mentions a chance encounter with Ernest Hemingway at a Berlin train station. The chance encounter reminds Sheean of Hemingway's single-minded focus and apparent lack of interest in larger issues of the world (280-281). Sheean wonders whether this self-centered attitude is responsible for Hemingway's literary success. Sheean also describes novelist Sinclair Lewis's systematic writing habits and his "hard work" (320-321). So we should take Sheean at his word, even though learning "to see…as straight as" possible and writing about it as accurately as one can are goals for a whole life (as the quote suggests). Nonetheless, one needs to begin someplace.

The quote—Rayna Prohme's advice—also suggests that writing can help Sheean connect with the world. Prohme advises Sheean (in their imaginary conversations) to write about issues that concern humanity as a whole (Sheean, *Personal History* 396). Elsewhere in *Personal History*, Sheean refers to his "desire to find some relationship between this one life and the millions of others into which it was cast" (185). He calls this desire a "search for sense." In fact, the book can be seen as a chronicle of his quest to find his purpose, his connection with the world. Nancy Cott describes *Personal History* as a "*bildungsroman*" (200). Deborah Cohen, a history scholar, also calls the book a "coming-of-age memoir" (xxi).

Sheean did not simply construct a metaphorical bridge between his past and present in *Personal History*. Consciously or not, he built a bridge to the future that helped him find and live his role as a journalist (as is often true with reflection). Tracy Kidder, a literary journalist, and Richard Todd, Kidder's editor, characterize memoirs in a similar vein: "The past becomes an assertion that your life is of the present and the future" (65).

Sheean found a form that suited him (Kronenberger) and would go on to write three more journalistic memoirs like *Personal History*, giving sweeping, personal, detailed, analytical, and candid accounts of significant and momentous historical events that he witnessed at close quarters. Sheean's choice of this form did not go unnoticed. Henry Seidel Canby mentions that since the publication of Sheean's book, "a dozen other ex-correspondents have followed his lead" (4). James Gray, a scholar of English, describes *Personal History* "as the archetype of all the books which took as their theme the education of the American as internationalist" (126). Kenneth Stweart, a contemporary journalist, acknowledges Sheean's contribution to their profession in these words: "Vincent Sheean awakened us as newspapermen to the long view" (313). The phrase "the long view" occurs a few times in the book (Sheean, *Personal History* 394). Sheean uses the term to characterize Michael Borodin, a Russian adviser to the "Left Kuomintang" (Isaacs 269) government in Hankow, China (Sheean,

Personal History 191), for his thoughtful and imperturbable outlook on situations and events. The phrase is also used in the book to suggest connections between individual events and larger, historical currents (Sheean, *Personal History* 204-205).

Taking a broader or a more holistic view of the world appealed to Sheean. He writes that events that interested him as a journalist were those involving "fundamental" questions a people faced (*Personal History* 187-188). Deborah Cohen, a scholar of history, sees *Personal History* in part as a "call for young people in the West to embrace the world's struggles" (xxi). Cohen also refers to Sheean's "One Worldism" (414), a belief in "peaceful cooperation between nations" (371). A few examples from *Personal History* may help us see Sheean's holistic view of the world better.

After returning from the Rif, where he met with the Riffian leader, Sheean asked the French prime minister, M. Painlevé, if he had any peace proposals for the Riffians (Sheean, *Personal History* 159). The prime minister did not have any such proposal, and Sheean left the prime minister's office feeling disappointed (159). In China, Sheean unsuccessfully tried to persuade one Mr. T. V. Soong, a Harvard-educated Chinese administrator, to return to Hankow to help the Kuomintang government manage its finances (Sheean, *Personal History* 194, 233-237). Once again, however, Sheean did not succeed. He even wondered if his desire to persuade Soong was in part motivated by his interests as a professional journalist. However, after some reflection, Sheean concluded that he had acted based on his personal convictions alone (237). He also felt guilty about this altruistic motive, remembering that he was a journalist and had to be unbiased.

As a journalist, Sheean tried to learn about people who were subjects of his stories. During his China visit, his employer, the *North American Newspaper Alliance*, wanted from him stories involving "personal adventures," an expression suggesting an assignment similar to that he carried out in the Rif a few years ago (Sheean, *Personal History* 247). In *Personal History*, Sheean responds to his employer's expectations in the following manner: "I had not gone to the Rif in pursuit of adventure, but to learn what I could about the Riffians and their country" (246). Sheean then has some fun at his employer's expectations from his reporting. He says that when he traveled eastward to meet with a Chinese warlord, he expected to run into problems in what was a strife-ridden country, which would have ironically provided him with an opportunity to satisfy his employer's demands. However, in a mock complaining tone, Sheean writes that he came across courteous Chinese people everywhere, which made it difficult for him to experience an adventure (Sheean, *Personal History* 248).

Sheean's commitment to and engagement in his reporting can be described as his "immersion" in his setting, a term literary journalism scholars use to denote "time spent on the job" (Sims, "The Literary Journalists" 10). Ted Conover, a literary journalist, explains that the term is understood as "spending significant amounts of time…engaged in daily exposure to your subjects and the problems they face" (16). *Personal History* has Sheean spending weeks in the Rif and months in China and former Palestine, meeting with people, empathizing with them when he is able to, taking calculated risks, observing things, using his wits, traveling, and, in general, absorbed in his settings. Immersion is similar to what Barbara Lounsberry calls "exhaustive research" (*The Art of Fact*, xiii-xiv). For example, Sheean tells the reader that he is dissatisfied with his writing about Persia, "a complex civilization" (*Personal History* 163), because his knowledge of the country is superficial. After reaching the Rif during his first trip, before he was able to meet the rebel leader Abd el-Krim, Sheean gathered detailed information about the Riffian army and government (103). In former Palestine, Sheean met with officials and citizens, Arabs, Jews, and British; read newspapers; wrote in a diary; and traveled to various locations and places.

Conover mentions "empathy" as an additional "benefit of immersion writing" (16). Although *Personal History* includes several instances of empathy shown by Sheean, one example stands out from the rest. It involves Abd el-Krim, the Riffian leader in northern Morocco whom Sheean visited twice amid his struggle against Spain and France to win freedom for his region. After "five years of almost unceasing war" (Harris 321), Abd el-Krim surrendered and was exiled in 1926 (Allard 23; Harris 225, 329), a development Sheean partly foresaw during his second and last visit to the leader (Sheean, *Personal History* 160-161). On a peaceful and sunny day, Sheean and Abd el-Krim are conversing placidly on a hilltop, looking down at the sea below. Carried away a bit by the moment and reminded of Monte Carlo, Sheean tells the rebel leader that his coastal region needs a casino (141). Although Sheean makes this remark innocently, if also thoughtlessly, he immediately realizes his error and regrets what he said. On his part, Abd el-Krim, suddenly pensive, replies that his region lacks many things. What he does not say—but Sheean and the readers understand—is that his homeland lacks freedom.

Sims states that "the literary quality of…works [of literary journalism] comes from the collision of worlds, from a confrontation with the symbols of another, real culture" ("The Literary Journalists" 4). He also mentions responsibility to one's research or reporting subjects as a characteristic of literary journalism (8). *Personal History* includes examples of both these qualities. After returning from his second tour of the Rif, Sheean felt happy when he realized that he was perhaps the only journalist to write about the Rif war from the Riffian perspective (Sheean, *Personal History* 156). Indeed, Sheean had undertaken a hazardous journey to the region to meet with the rebel leader, unlike many of his peers. In keeping with the responsibility he felt toward the subjects of his reporting, Sheean felt frustrated when he encountered inaccurate information in the press about the Rif struggle (117-118).

Personal History includes accounts of Sheean's visits to a number of European countries, Morocco, Persia (now Iran), China, Russia, and former Palestine. He worked for various employers during these visits. During his first Rif trip, he was a foreign correspondent for the European edition of the Chicago *Tribune* published from Paris (Sheean, *Personal History* 116). During the second trip, he worked for the *North American Newspaper Alliance* (119). For his Persia visit, he signed a contract with a magazine called *Asia* (162-163). After leaving Russia, Sheean briefly worked for the *Paris Times* (306). To go to former Palestine, Sheean got a reporting assignment from *The New Palestine* (335). However, later, due to an ethical conflict, he returned the advance he had received from the publication (343). His "arrangement" (364) with the *North American Newspaper Alliance* also ended due to a controversy his reporting from Palestine created (376).

Sheean reached Palestine on June 25, 1929, after getting an advance of five hundred dollars from *The New Palestine*, a magazine supporting Zionism, a growing movement at the time for a Jewish homeland (Sheean, *Personal History* 335-336; Alterman 27-28). The editor had agreed to a condition by Sheean that he would not write anything amounting to propaganda. Nonetheless, in July, an Arab newspaper accused Sheean of being a paid journalist (Sheean, *Personal History* 342-343). Disturbed by this allegation, Sheean returned the advance to *The New Palestine* and refused a further amount that he had been promised. In August, Sheean witnessed the violent clashes between Arabs and Jews due to a dispute involving the Wailing Wall in Jerusalem (Winder 6). The conflict spread to other parts of what was then Palestine. Although he continued to meet with his Jewish friends and helped the U.S. State Department account for Jewish Americans (Sheean, *Personal History* 376-377), he came to blame supporters of Zionism for the conflict (367). He also felt angry and disappointed with the Arabs and the British, the former for their extreme reaction and the latter for their lack of preparedness. Some news stories that he sent from Palestine sparked protests by Jewish readers in America (375). These reactions led to a parting between Sheean and the *North American Newspaper Alliance*. Sheean had also asked the organization to end his contract (375-376). Although this chapter does not analyze Sheean's reporting from Palestine, it may be briefly noted that the crux of his account of the events has found scholarly support.

Alex Winder, a scholar of history and the Middle East, recalls Vincent Sheean's visit to Palestine and states that "the violence took place in the context of rising Palestinian frustration over the [British] Mandate's Jewish National Home Policy" (6). In his recent book *We Are Not One: A History of America's Fight over Israel*, Eric Alterman, a journalist and a scholar of English, notes, "In their euphoria, the Zionists ignored the [Balfour] declaration's caveat that in the event of the creation of any…homeland, 'the civil and religious rights of existing non-Jewish communities in Palestine' had to be respected" (28). Alterman mentions "Arab riots" of 1920, 1929, and 1936.

In *Personal History*, Sheean's integration of narratives about disparate places gives the work its distinctive literary quality. R. L. Duffus, a contemporary reviewer of the book for *The New York Times*, describes *Personal History* as "a remarkable achievement in synthesis" ("Mr. Sheean's Post-War" 1). The book reminds one of Lounsberry's statement that "the narrative form and structure disclose the writer's artistry" (*The Art of Fact* xv).

According to Jack Hart, a journalism scholar and a journalist, "a narrative… proceeds through a series of scenes carefully selected to tell the story" (100). *Personal History* includes frequent stories along with "historical narrative" (Wolfe 31), description, reflection, and commentary. Although Wolfe does not define what he means by "historical narrative," the term suggests a traditional exposition relying on "telling" rather than "showing," or, as journalism scholar R. Thomas Berner puts it, a "summary" rather than a "scene" (5). John Hollowell, a literary journalism scholar, translates the term as a "historical summary" or "a summary of the events" (25-26).

One should note, however, that Wolfe admitted that "he could only make *The Electric Kool-Aid Acid Test* and *The Right Stuff* work by abandoning strict adherence to these techniques [those included in his definition of New Journalism, such as reliance on scenes as much as possible] in favor of summary narration and exposition" (Hellman 22). Importantly, Hellman summarizes an argument made by Barbara Foley, a scholar of English, about Wolfe's definition of literary (new) journalism: "there are serious logical difficulties in defining a genre by 'quantification,' for it immediately places works having only some of these devices in an ambiguous area" (22).

Given these problems with Wolfe's definition, I will not attempt to make any fine estimate of the extent of scenes (or stories) versus that of historical summary in Sheean's books. However, because there is a wide agreement among literary journalism scholars that scenes or stories are a core characteristic of the form (Connery *A Sourcebook*; Kramer, "Breakable Rules"; Sims *True Stories*), I will treat Sheean's books that include more scenes or stories as having a better claim to literary journalism. Books with more story-like elements have a greater claim to the form compared to books that include more "non-narrative elements"—such as commentary and description (Georgakopoulou and Goutsos 71)—and historical summary.

Scenes "grab the reader and pull her in, making her want to know what will happen next" (Hertz 138). They enable a writer to "swiftly locate the reader in place and time" (Lounsberry, *Writing Creative* 78). Scenes also help readers to "experience something directly related to what the account is about" (Warnock xix). Describing scenes, R. Thomas Berner states that "the more a writer *shows* a story happening the more the writer can compel a reader to read on" (4-5, emphasis mine). According to Chris Baldick, a scholar of English, "a scene normally represents actions happening in one place at one time" (323). R. Thomas Berner's description of the term "scene" seems broader and more flexible, whereas Baldick's interpretation of the term seems a bit restrictive. As mentioned earlier, Jack Hart's conception of a scene is that of a unit in a story.

Because at least two of the three narratives involving action in *Personal History* that I analyze reflect events that do not occur "in one place" (as Baldick appears to require of a scene), I will use in my analysis the more common term "stories" to differentiate narratives showing action and dialogue from those that are mainly historical (or a historical summary). Indeed, stories, too, comprise scenes and summaries. As has been noted, literary journalism scholars commonly use the term "stories" to describe this form (Connery *A Sourcebook*; Kramer "Breakable Rules"; Hartsock *A History*). In fact, a literary journalism text by Mark Kramer and Wendy Call is titled *Telling True Stories* (xv).

My main argument in this chapter is that cohesive integration of varied narratives (stories and historical narratives) in *Personal* History—its "remarkable synthesis" (Duffus, "Mr. Sheean's Post-War" 1)—is due to four factors: The first is the linear, chronological structure of the book. Simple and short chapter titles form the second factor. The book's frequent stories—narratives showing action and comprising a number of scenes (Hart; Berner)—are the third factor. These stories are accompanied by historical narratives or summaries (telling or recounting events versus showing them through characters, action, and dialogue). I further suggest that the greater the extent of stories in a chapter, each of which deals with a topic area, the more effectively the chapter contributes to the book's cohesion. Stories succeed in imparting cohesion to a book because they involve readers and help them experience a more seamless reading: "I couldn't put it down" (Hart 15). Hart elaborates on this experience: "A compelling story must immerse readers in another world....Writers accomplish that kind of diversion by combining strong action lines with artful scene-setting, reproducing realities where readers can join the story's characters." Hence, stories strengthen cohesion and readers' engagement in a book. Finally, crisp sentences providing information constitute the fourth factor in helping to integrate a variety of narratives. Of course, the sentences also perform other tasks (for example, expressing sorrow, anger, humor, or sarcasm). In what follows, I explain each of the four factors.

In addition to the four factors, I contend that the narrator's "presence" (Gornick 4) helps in achieving the book's cohesion. This presence shows itself through the authorial "I"—the "narrative persona in first-person nonfiction" (Conover 117)—in the book's narratives (stories and historical narratives or summaries). In fact, the narrator's presence pervades the entire book, including in description, reflection, and commentary, a quality literary critic Vivian Gornick describes as "the merger between the narrator and subject" (128).

The narrator's presence and crisp, informative sentences contribute to an even, consistent tone in the book, which facilitates reading. In her book *The Artful Edit*, editor Susan Bell credits "Continuity of tone" with helping to achieve cohesion and flow (87). Although she does not discuss Sheean's books, she asserts that "continuity of tone. . . matters as much to nonfiction" (86). In his 1935 review, Duffus remarks on the readability of *Personal History* in this way: "it will be a rare reader who doesn't follow [the book] to the end" ("Mr. Sheean's Post-War" 1).

Chronological Structure and Simple Chapter Titles

The book follows a linear, chronological course. According to Tracy Kidder and Richard Todd, "telling stories in chronological order has a distinguished lineage in Western literature, which includes, among others, all the classical narratives and most novels well into the twentieth century" (41). Their advice to writers: "Don't mess with chronology unless you have a good reason" (40). Hart acknowledges the elementary nature of a chronological structure (23). In a book having numerous narratives spanning several geographies and cultures, a chronological or linear structure gives readers a "straightforward" path (Kidder and Todd 42), facilitating the book's reading and enjoyment.

In addition, although dates are frequently mentioned, the book does not overburden a reader with them. For example, years are mentioned only occasionally. This strategy also helps integrate disparate narratives (stories and historical narratives) because the reader experiences a more seamless, integrated narration. Frequent dates would draw the attention of readers, making them notice and perhaps accentuate variations among the narratives.

A lesser emphasis on dates also makes the book seem more like fiction and less like a memoir (a feature of the book highlighted by Malcolm Cowley in his 1935 review). Nonetheless, it is still possible to construct a timeline of the events narrated in the book.

The book begins with an account of Sheean's years at the University of Chicago (1917-1921); the second chapter is a long narrative about his early journalistic jobs in New York and Paris, including his reporting trips to Germany, Italy, Spain, and Switzerland (1921-1924); the third and fourth chapters tell the story of Sheean's two visits to the Rif region in northern Morocco to learn about the struggle of the Riffian people against their colonial rulers, Spain and, later, France (1924-1925); the fifth chapter is about Sheean's brief tour of Persia (1926); the sixth chapter narrates significant events in the book that take place in China and Russia (1927); the seventh chapter puts Sheean in key European cities and the United States (1928-29); and the last chapter narrates Sheean's experiences in former Palestine, before his return to the U.S. via Athens, Greece (1929).

Like the book's simple structure, the chapter titles of the book are simple and short, with an eye perhaps on readers' involvement in the book. The modest titles do not distract and seem to encourage readers to find out what a chapter will include. For example, chapter two, dealing with Sheean's nascent journalistic career, is called "Journalism." Chapter five is called "Desert Gardens," a synecdoche for Persia because Sheean makes some observations about the country's passion for gardens. Chapter six, involving China and Russia, is titled "Revolution," referring to the events Sheean witnessed in China and, in a different way, in Russia; people with whom he spent time in both countries; and the connection of the events in the two countries to his own life. The laconic chapter titles, often a word or two, contribute to the book's cohesion because they often look alike.

Stories with an "Embodied" Narrator

Stories—narratives showing action involving characters and dialogue (Fontaine & Glavin, Jr.)—in *Personal History* make it fiction-like. In fact, in his 1935 review of the book for *The New Republic*, Malcolm Cowley writes, "This autobiography, with a few names changed to give it the appearance of fiction, would certainly rank among the good novels of this decade" (50). Writing about literary journalism, Sims states that "reading a nonfiction book that tells gripping stories with emotional complexity may be an experience similar to reading a novel" (*True Stories* 2).

I argue that frequent stories help with integration of varied narratives (stories and historical narratives or summaries) in *Personal History*. How does the overall narrative identity of the book—recall Cowley's 1935 remark about the book being potentially a novel with a few changes—contribute to its cohesion? A major part of the answer is stories, with the author's "I" guiding them in a restrained manner. This last point—let's call it a modest "I" for lack of a better term—is suggested by R.L. Duffus in his *New York Times* review: "There is very little here that is acutely personal, and self-consciousness appears only when Mr. Sheean interrupts the narrative to point out that he is lacking in personal courage (one is sure he is wrong about that), or to intimate that he has been somewhat of a failure" ("Mr. Sheean's Post-War" 1). Gornick writes about her own discovery of a modest "I" in one of her works, written with a "created persona" (23): "*I was to use myself only to clarify the argument, develop the analysis, push the story forward*" (10, my emphasis). Sheean's use of the first person pronoun in *Personal History* is similar.

Conversely, as noted earlier, the narratives—not to mention "non-narrative modes" (Georgakopoulou & Goutsos 66)—in *Personal History* are imbued with the narrator's presence (not an obtrusive or dominating one), so the reader finds the narrator as a common character throughout the book. In fact, literary critic F. K. Stanzel calls the first-person narrator of autobiographical works an "embodied" character (90). As we will see later, this presence, as conceptualized by Gornick and Stanzel, also contributes to the book's cohesion despite its various narratives (stories and historical narratives).

Although the book has many stories—narratives showing action involving characters and dialogue (Fontaine & Glavin, Jr.)—three stories from Sheean's two Rif expeditions and a story about the last days of Rayna Prohme, a young American friend of Sheean, are particularly well-crafted.

Sheean's visits to the Rif region in northern Morocco arose because of an ongoing war between Spain and the Riffian people, led by Abd el-Krim. Walter B. Harris, a contemporary British reporter, succinctly explains the basis for the conflict: "[Spain] has…the agreement with France that she was to occupy and administer a section of Northern Morocco extending from the Algerian frontier to a spot a little south of the town of Laraiche on the Atlantic coast, including the whole Northern coast-line with the exception of Tangier" (9). The Rif was part of this territory to be administered by Spain (Harris 43-44). Harris describes the Rifis, inhabitants of this area, as a Berber people or those descending from both Berbers and Arabs (21-22). What began as a war with Spain became a war with both Spain and France toward its concluding phase, in 1925 (Harris 210-212).

Sheean went to Morocco the first time toward the end of 1924 (Sheean, *Personal History* 84). There he met with Primo de Rivera, the Spanish dictator, who told him about Spain's changing war plans (85-86) against the Riffian fighters. Wanting to know more about the Riffian war, Sheean asked Primo de Rivera if it was possible to talk to Abd el-Krim, the leader of the Riffian struggle (87). The Spanish leader dismissed this idea. However, Sheean was not discouraged and decided to find a way to meet the rebel leader.

A young man named Mohammed ben Haddu agreed to take Sheean to the rebel leader (91). On their way to the Rif, Sheean and the incompetent Haddu were helped by a French officer, who provided them with an experienced guide (93). To avoid attracting attention, Sheean dressed like an Arab (94). On their difficult and exhausting journey, they came across a man murdered by local tribesmen (95). After trudging across a hilly terrain through the night, Sheean fell asleep on a bare rock in the early morning hours. However, shortly afterward, Sheean, Haddu, and another guide, a fellow called Mohammed of Midar, were detained by men of an "Arab tribe," called Metalsa, who lived in hillside caves (96-98). After a few days of captivity and having been cheated out of his money by Haddu, Sheean persuaded his abductor—one Caïd Hamid (102)—to let him continue his journey to see the Riffian leader (101). At last, Sheean reached his destination and met with Abd el-Krim (103). He also collected information about the Riffian army and government. A confident Abd el-Krim told Sheean about his demand for complete independence from Spain (105). On his way back, assisted by Abd el-Krim's men, Sheean met a German man who by a twist of fate had found himself in the Rif (107-108). He told Sheean many stories, and, as he discovered later, a falsehood or two. Thus ended Sheean's first journey to the Rif.

According to author and journalism scholar Jack Hart, a story structure—or, what he calls, a "narrative arc"—comprises the following stages (22). The first stage is "exposition," which introduces characters, the setting, and so on—background information that readers need to understand a story (24). Toward the end of the exposition, a story writer includes an "inciting incident," which Hart explains as "the event that sets the whole story in motion" (28). The second stage is "rising action," which forms the "bulk" of a story. This stage shows a story in progress. "Any development that spins the story off in a new direction" is called a "plot point." The third stage is "crisis," which is when a story comes "to a head" and "everything hangs in the balance" (32). Crisis marks "the peak of a narrative arc" (34) and may include a "point of insight" at some stage, "an event that sets up the resolution" (35). Stage four is "climax," which is "the event—or series of events—that resolves the crisis" (36). The last stage is called "falling action" or "denouement," where "things wind down" (37). A story structure based on these stages from Sheean's first Rif voyage is depicted in Table 2.1 below.

Table 2.1: A Story Structure of the First Rif Journey Based on Jack Hart's Story Framework

Stages of a Story	Events
Exposition	• A historical narrative involving Sheean's time in Paris, France; Madrid, Spain; Tangier and Tetuan, Morocco; in Spain, Morocco was an urgent topic (Sheean, *Personal History* 83-86) • *Inciting incident*: A meeting with the Spanish dictator Primo de Rivera in Tetuan, in which Sheean asks if a visit to the Rif is possible. The dictator dismisses the idea, spurring Sheean and strengthening his conviction that he must find a way to go into the Rif (87).
Rising action	• Sheean arrives in Tangier, encounters "delays" (88). • He takes a car to the "French Zone," the area in Morocco controlled by the French (88). • Sheean arrives in Oudjda, Morocco (90). • He travels to a border town in neighboring Algeria to look for a guide for the journey into the Rif. • With Mohammed ben Haddu, a young Arab whose father was originally sought by Sheean as a guide on his journey into the Rif, Sheean begins his Rif journey; he reaches Oudjda, then Taourirt, the point from which people headed into the Rif (91). • A French officer called Gabrielli arranges for an experienced guide for Sheean, Haddu being seen as not up to the task; The new guide accompanying Sheean is one Mohammed of Midar. Sheean's small group leaves Taourirt (93-94).
Crisis	• After being stopped in pre-dawn hours and Sheean falling asleep on a rock, Sheean follows Haddu to hillside caves in which Metalsa tribesmen live; Sheean realizes he is detained by the tribesmen; Mohammed of Midar, who is being allowed to leave, warns Sheean that his fate is uncertain (95-98). • *Point of insight*: Sheean finds a tribesman who can speak Spanish (101); the man suggests to Sheean to write to Gabrielli, the French officer, for money, so that he can resume his voyage (after Haddu escapes with Sheean's money).
Climax	• With what gifts he can muster, Sheean persuades his captor, the chief of the tribe, to allow him to send letters to Gabrielli and Abd el-Krim (whose authority the Metalsa tribesmen accept) to continue his journey to the Rif. Sheean leaves for the Rif (101-103).
Falling action / denouement	• Sheean arrives in Ajdir, the Riffian capital (103). • He meets Abd el-Krim, the Riffian leader (104). • He returns through the area controlled by Abd el-Krim on his advice (105). • Sheean reaches Tangier (113).

The Making of the Seeker and His Craft

As can be seen in Table 2.1, the story from Sheean's first Rif trip appears to follow the structure suggested by Hart. Two stories from Sheean's second Rif visit seem more fiction-like and dramatic compared to the story from the first Rif journey.

When Sheean returned to the Rif in September 1925, Spain and France had joined forces to defeat the Riffian fighters (Sheean, *Personal History* 120-129). Harris writes that mutual suspicions and threats eventually brought Riffian fighters into a direct conflict with France (211-212). Just before Sheean's arrival, the French and the Spanish had agreed to "cooperate" (244). The increased military activity by the two European powers made Sheean's journey difficult (Sheean, *Personal History* 129). Again, Sheean found a guide who led him into the remote, war-torn region (127). As he had done during his first journey, Sheean wore an Arab dress to avoid standing out as a foreigner (126). On the way to his destination, Sheean and his guide were joined by one Abdullah, a smuggler (129). Abdullah constantly misbehaved and cursed Sheean, who became afraid because Abdullah had a knife and threatened to use it (130). Additionally, Sheean's guide—Mahdani—had disappeared (131-132). Finally, finding an opportunity, Sheean fled from Abdullah and hid in a field, bracing himself against Abdullah's frantic search accompanied by angry shouts and curses (130-134).

Safely reaching his destination after this ordeal, Sheean met with Abd el-Krim in a mountainous abode (136). On the way to the Riffian leader's home, Sheean had to protect himself from Spanish warplanes (135-136). Later, Sheean saw Abd el-Krim demonstrate his courage by firing at enemy fighter planes from near the entrance to the cave to which he and Sheean had temporarily retired (138-139). On his return journey from the Rif, Sheean seems to have contracted Malaria (144). An African American volunteer, and a later deserter, in the French foreign army helped him recover (146-147). Finally, after many days of grueling journey, Sheean returned to safety in Tangier (153).

Table 2.2 shows the structures of the two stories from Sheean's second Rif visit based on Jack Hart's framework. The story of the second Rif journey reads as two stories: Sheean going into the Rif and his return journey.

Table 2.2: Two Story Structures of the Second Rif Journey Based on Jack Hart's Story Framework

Stages of a Story	Events
Exposition	- Sheean rests in Tangier at the end of his first Rif visit, then goes to Madrid, Spain, and meets with the Spanish dictator; returns to Paris; then, he is fired from his job over a misunderstanding. Although he feels bad about it, his firing does not read like a crisis. It might have become one later, however (Sheean, *Personal History* 114-116).
- Sheean leaves for New York, writes a book about his first Rif journey (117-118).
- *Inciting incident*: While in New York, amid growing frustration, Sheean accidentally meets Merian Cooper, a former journalist who also fought for Poland against the Soviet Union. Cooper takes Sheean to the office of the *North American Newspaper Alliance*, who would like Sheean to reprise his Rif visit. This assignment starts Sheean on his second Rif visit (118-119).
Rising action	- Sheean arrives in Tangier. A bit of a historical narrative. He asks Ali, who is a brother of Mohammed bel Hadj (a Riffian soldier who accompanied Sheean on his return journey during the first excursion into the Rif), to arrange for his visit to the Rif. Ali promises to help through his mother-in-law (119-121).
- Sheean meets with his guide, arranged by Ali's mother-in-law; requests a British telegraph official to send his telegrams containing news stories to his employer (123).
- Sheean follows Mahdani, his guide, through a beach to go to Ali's mother-in-law's house. Then, they—Sheean and his guide—start for the Rif (125-127).
- After sleeping in a ditch on the way, Sheean reaches Bohrabish (128).
- Sheean and Mahdani leave Bohrabish at 6 p.m. for Dar ben Karish. Abdullah, a smuggler from Sheshuan, joins them (129).
Crisis	- Mahdani disappears. Sheean is forced to go on with Abdullah, who misbehaves and threatens Sheean. Finally, fearing for his life and seeing an opportunity, Sheean decides to flee. He hides in a cornfield, where Abdullah comes looking for Sheean. At one point, Abdullah comes near the spot where Sheean is hiding (131-132).
- *Point of insight*: When Sheean and Abdullah come near a field with a stream, Abdullah orders Sheean to get some water. This demand of Abdullah provides Sheean with an opportunity to escape (132).
Climax	- Having passed the night hiding in a cornfield, Sheean cautiously emerges in the morning at the approach of a group of men going in the direction where he needs to go to reach the Rif. Sheean joins the group (133).
Falling action / denouement	- Sheean reunites with Mahdani, halts at Targhzuit (133-134).
- Sheean starts for the final stretch of his journey (135).
- Sheean and Mahdani, joined by a few others, encounter Spanish fighter planes and their bombardment. This point, too, appears to be a crisis. However, Sheean tells us that this experience lasted about an hour (135-136). Thus, this incident appears to be a situation of risk, something Sheean often faced in his trips to the Rif.

		• Sheean meets with and talks to Abd el-Krim, briefly visits the scene of fighting with Abd el-Krim (136-141).
Exposition (again, another story in the second Rif visit)		• Sheean explains that his contract required him to return to Tangier, and he wanted to see fighting in southern Morocco before returning. He leaves to go and see a tribe called the Branès (142).
		• *Inciting incident:* Sheean had to return from his Rif trip anyway. However, his contract terms required him to conclude his tour of the Rif in a certain amount of time. Eager to meet his commitments as a reporter, Sheean wanted to travel to the south to get a picture of the war there (142). It is possible that if he were simply required to return after meeting with the Riffian leader, his subsequent journey may have been different.
Rising action		• Sheean wanted to go to the territory of the Branes. However, he does not reach this area. Instead, feeble and hungry, he is at Targuist (142-143).
		• Based on Sidi Hassan's advice, Sheean decides to cancel his plans to go to the south and instead return to Tangier via Sheshuan (144).
Crisis		• Sheean is sick with malaria. He does not have a guide or a mule. He does not get proper rest or food. He loses the sense of time. The journey becomes a test of endurance (144-145).
		• *Point of insight:* After a painful journey in which he became seriously ill, Sheean reaches a village he recognizes. There, completely by chance, Sheean meets an African American young man who joined and then left the French foreign army. Sheean asks for his assistance (146).
Climax		• Wesley Williams, the African American, brings eggs and milk for Sheean, which he gratefully accepts. Williams also suggests an idiosyncratic but a quick way (yelling) that helps reduce Sheean's fever (146-147).
		• Sheean finds a mule and a guide or a muleteer for his journey to Sheshuan (147).
Falling action / denouement		• Sheean somehow reaches Sheshuan, a Riffi official looks after him; two Italian adventurers are good company to Sheean (147-149).
		• Sheean leaves for Tangier, falls down on his way and near the destination on a ground watched by Spanish soldiers, and is rescued by one of the Italians he met at Sheshuan (151-152). Although Sheean's fall and his unwillingness to rise again due to exhaustion and pain seems to be a crisis, his Italian rescuer quickly came to his aid. Thus, the incident appears more like a particularly difficult situation.
		• Sheean reaches Tangier safely, invites the Italian rescuer—Alfredo Morea—for dinner (150-153).
		• Sheean meets with various people after his return. He has earned fame due to his reporting. Among others, he also meets with French politicians to discuss the Riffian struggle (156-157).

Tables 2.1 and 2.2 confirm our intuitive sense that the Rif narratives contain stories "letting you see the people acting out the event" (Fontaine & Glavin, Jr. 144). The stories read novelistically or in a "cinematic" fashion (Hertz 114), as if "transport[ing]" (Denning 59) the reader to northern Morocco in the second decade of the twentieth century. So involved may a reader become that she may

look up places and people on Google, fascinated by the enormous canvas the world history offers. As Gornick writes of the eulogist she heard and remembered, "The story here was not either the speaker or the doctor per se; it was what happened to each of them in the other's company" (5-6). Gornick might have written these words for Sheean's *Personal History*.

The Rif stories include some dialogues, but, as Lounsberry points out, they are not "essential" to a story (*The Art of Fact* xv). Indeed, it is difficult to see Sheean use extensive dialogues in these stories given the language barrier between him and many of the characters in the stories, people with whom he came into contact. Sheean is able to use rudimentary Arabic and Spanish to talk to people, but one gets an impression that their communication must have been basic and aided in part by nonverbal cues. Still, dialogues in these stories provide for revelatory moments or move the story forward, such as brief conversations between Sheean and Abd el-Krim; between Sheean and the Spanish dictator Primo de Rivera; between Sheean and Wesley Williams, the African American recruit in the French army who saves Sheean from his bad illness; between Sheean and the brother of Mohammed bel Hadj, the Riffian soldier whom Sheean enormously admired; and between Sheean and Alfredo Morea, a young Italian politician whom Sheean meets in Sheshuan after his Malaria-afflicted return.

At times, when there is no dialogue, there is effective nonverbal communication: "glowering Abdullah"; "the smuggler growled and snarled and beat my mule across the rump"; "behaved like a slave driver" (Sheean, *Personal History* 131). There is also action: Sheean's apprehensive trek under the baleful gaze of Abduallah, Sheean's continuous assessment of the threat, his desperate escape with Abdullah just a little behind, his fear at Abdullah's approach, and his cautious refuge in a field before emerging in the morning.

Tracy Kidder and Richard Todd contend that "more than any other aspect of storytelling, the successful rendering of characters depends on the reader" (30). They explain that "the goal is to get characters off the page and into the reader's imagination. When this happens, transport follows." There are several characters in the Rif stories who seem like people that readers may know in their own lives or are able to imagine. Perhaps the most successful character is the thoughtful and determined Abd el-Krim. In the story of the second Rif journey, Sheean portrays the Riffian leader vividly. The reader can see this humble and dignified man sitting on the floor in a dark room, welcoming Sheean with a soft and brief greeting.

The Riffian leader seems familiar, even if different in many ways. Sheean and Abd el-Krim talk as friends, candidly, with trust. When Abd el-Krim notices that Sheean is not wearing shoes, he gets up and tries to find a pair of shoes from a collection of enemy soldiers' shoes (Sheean, *Personal History* 137). However,

The Making of the Seeker and His Craft   51

when no pair fits Sheean's large feet, the Riffian leader chuckles, just like any other friend would have given a similar situation. The Riffian leader talks to Sheean about the ongoing war (137-138), as if sharing confidential information with a trusted friend (granted that the Riffian leader also wanted the press to report his perspective on the war). On his part, Sheean notices his friend's "limp" when Abd el-Krim hurries Sheean to a hideout on being warned of an air attack (138). Based on these details, it is difficult for a reader to reject the idea that an American journalist and a Moroccan rebel can understand each other. The fact that these two men are from vastly different cultures and societies does not seem to matter that much.

Another memorable character in the Rif stories is Mohammed bel Hadj, the Riffian soldier who helped Sheean return to Tangier—a neutral area under the colonial arrangement (Sheean, *Personal History* 84)—after his first voyage to the Rif region. Sheean states that "Hadj was taking as much care of me as if I had been a set of China" (112). The gallant soldier died during the Rif war. Sheean remembers Mohammed bel Hadj toward the end of the second Rif chapter, "And the bones of my friend Mohammed bel Hadj...must long ago have added their pinch of dust....The traveler in such regions...does well to wrap his turban...to keep it out of eyes and throat; it will sting no less for being the dust of an honest man" (161).

The story of Rayna Prohme—a young American woman and a friend of Sheean who worked for the "Left Kuomintang" (Isaacs 269) government in Hankow, China, before moving to Russia and dying there of encephalitis (Sheean, *Personal History* 300)—is poignantly told in *Personal History*. Sheean, who was enamored of her, dedicated the book to her. Rayna, the reader will recall, "speaks" to Sheean and advises him to see clearly and write exactly.

Sheean met Rayna in China around May 1927 (213). Originally from Chicago, Rayna studied at the University of Illinois (215). She and her husband, Bill Prohme, were in Hankow where Rayna "work[ed] for Borodin," a Russian advisor to the government (213). She edited the government's paper called *The People's Tribune* (214, 229). A *New York Times* journalist introduced Rayna and Sheean (213-214).

In July 1927, shortly before the fall of the Hankow government—because the communists supporting the "Left Kuomintang" found themselves without allies (Isaacs 269)—Sheean left for eastern China (Sheean, *Personal History* 247). Sheean writes that the Hankow government seemed to promise another communist experiment such as the 1917 November revolution in Russia (217). However, because of contradictions, China did not see a repeat of Russia (Isaacs).

Rayna Prohme saw Sheean off at the train station (Sheean, *Personal History* 255). She mentioned that they may meet in Moscow. Sheean reached Moscow on September 18 and found Rayna at Metropol Hotel (261-263). They spent a few days together, talking, walking, or going to a theater. By the end of the month, needing money, Sheean had to leave for England (272-278).

Sheean returned to Moscow on November 7, 1927 (281). Rayna had rented a couple of rooms for him (282); her own apartment was next to Sheean's. In London, Cambridge, and Berlin, Sheean had a chance to reflect, and his outlook on the communist revolution of Russia had changed. Sheean realized his own incapacity to accept communism and dreaded the possibility that Rayna might sacrifice her life in pursuit of this ideology (285-286). Rayna and Sheean talked to their landlady and went to the Red Square to see the tenth-anniversary celebrations of the Russian Revolution (282). Over the next few days, Sheean and Rayna argued repeatedly over her decision to join the communist party (285-287). On November 12, Sheean treated Rayna to a dinner at Grand Hotel, an ironic gesture deliberately chosen by him given her decision to join the communist party (291). On that day, Rayna fainted (292). Her condition continued to worsen, and, once, when she had passed out, Sheean carried her in his arms to Hotel Metropol (294-295). Sheean asked a German doctor to come and see Rayna, who trusted this doctor (296-297). Sheean listened to Rayna reminisce about her childhood when she felt better (298). Rayna Prohme died on November 21, 1927 (299). She was cremated on November 24. The next day, Sheean left for Berlin (302).

Table 2.3 shows the story structure of the last days of Rayna Prohme's life based on Jack Hart's story framework. The story depicted in the structure begins immediately after Sheean's return to Moscow on November 7.

Table 2.3: The Story Structure of Rayna Prohme's Last Days Based on Jack Hart's Story Framework

Stages of a Story	Events
Exposition	• Sheean and Rayna visit the house in which Rayna has rented rooms for them both, independent but adjacent (Sheean, *Personal History* 281-282). • They visit the Red Square to watch the events celebrating the tenth anniversary of the Russian Revolution (283). • Sheean is critical of the celebrations, an impression Rayna does not fully share; she notices his changed behavior. • More than once, Sheean and Rayna talk—argue—until early morning (285). • *Inciting incident*: Rayna has recurrent headaches (286); she does not know the reason for it. [*In a book containing several letters by Rayna Prohme by Baruch Hirson and Arthur J. Knodel, there is a letter from Rayna to her husband, William, dated October 26, 1927. In this letter, Rayna refers to her "incessant" headaches. She does not seem to be aware of its reason or cause (132).*] However, this condition will lead to her death in the next few days.
Rising action	• Sheean and Rayna meet with some American friends: Anna Louise, Lewis [Louis?] Fischer, and Dorothy Thompson (Sheean, *Personal History* 288).

The Making of the Seeker and His Craft 53

	• Full of forebodings, Sheean drinks Vodka (290).
	• Sheean and Rayna have their final argument, which lasts through most of the night (291). Sheean decides to leave Moscow, and Rayna would visit the Lenin Institute. Sheean asks her to join him at the Grand Hotel for a farewell dinner. He wants her to wear a dress Soong Ching-ling (Mme Sun Yat-sen) gifted her in China. Rayna agrees but says that she will need to put on an overcoat once they come out of the hotel.
	• On the day of the dinner, in the morning, Rayna faints (292).
	• In the evening, at the dinner, Sheean and Rayna dance together. Back at the table, Sheean "pound[s]" Rayna's shoulders to stress to Rayna that she is making a big mistake in deciding to join the communist party. Rayna distances herself a little, laughs, but reminds Sheean that he is hurting her shoulders (292).
	• Sheean and Rayna go to an event organized by the Congress of Friends of the Soviet Union. At the event, foreign communists are being honored. Rayna is moved by the ceremony. This reaction irritates Sheean who makes a snide remark about one of the honorees, angering Rayna. Sheean goes to the Grand Hotel to drink Vodka before retiring for the night (293-294).
Crisis	• Rayna Prohme loses consciousness at Hôtel de l'Europe. Sheean has to physically carry her to Metropol Hotel. She loses consciousness again (294-295).
	• A Russian doctor arrives with his assistants (295). He gives her ether, which does not agree with her body (296).
	• Sheean moves out of rented rooms and into Hotel Savoy (296).
	• Rayna is conscious again. She refuses to go to the Kremlin Hospital (296).
	• Sheean goes out to look for a doctor because Rayna wants one whom she "could trust" (296).
	• Sheean goes to journalist Walter Duranty's house where he meets another American, Bruce Hopper, who suggests Dr. Linck, connected with the German embassy (296).
	• Dr. Linck forbids political discussions considering Rayna's condition. Rayna feels a bit better and talks to Sheean about her childhood (297-298).
	• Rayna is apprehensive after the doctor examines her and asks her questions to see if she can think properly. Sheean briefly reassures Rayna (298-299).
	• Sheean sits beside Rayna, who is silent. A nurse arrives on Dr. Linck's advice (299).
	• Dr. Linck gives a stark prognosis. Sheean returns to Hotel Savoy and falls asleep in early morning hours (299).
	• [The story does not appear to have a "point of insight," "an event that sets up the resolution of the crisis" (Hart 35). Although Dr. Linck's stark prognosis can be seen as one, Sheean is mentally unprepared to see the information clearly (Sheean, *Personal History* 297).]
Climax	• Rayna Prohme dies on November 21, 1927. Her autopsy shows the cause of her death to be encephalitis (299-300).
Falling action / denouement	• Rayna is cremated on November 24. Sheean is present for it (299-301).
	• Borodin comes to speak with Sheean (301).
	• Sheean leaves Moscow for Berlin (302).

The story of Rayna Prohme's last days is narrated with details that occurred and bits of dialogue. The arguments between Sheean and Rayna are not given as dialogues. They are described generally, with brief exchanges between the two. For example, Sheean brings up a point about ethical lapses by communists and asks Rayna if she could resort to similar tactics (Sheean, *Personal History* 287). He also charges her with superficial attraction to communist revolutions and revolutionaries (287-288). But he is also aware that his assumptions about Rayna Prohme are groundless. Rayna deflects such arguments, gently chiding Sheean for saying such things (287-288). Later, when Rayna is sick, fainting and losing consciousness, elaborate speech on her part is not possible, so it is not surprising that we do not see detailed dialogues. Besides, given the gravity of what happened to her in her last days, a narration of most everything that occurred seems preferable to a few dialogues, which may not have occurred except when they argued (also assuming that Sheean preferred to write dialogues or could write them with great skill—remember his self-admonition to improve his writing?).

Toward the end of the story, Sheean's narration acquires a bare-bones and grave quality. Reflecting in a later chapter, Sheean finds Rayna Prohme's death mystifying, the process leading up to it ineluctable (Sheean, *Personal History* 304-305). Sheean characterizes his relationship with Rayna as "love resolved into the largest terms" (261-263). Her personality appealed to him, which he refers to on several occasions (215-216), as did her outlook on life or the world (265-270). While calling her a "pure flame" (272), he disagreed with her about communism (231, 285-287). Next, I discuss the fourth factor contributing to the book's cohesive narration: crisp, informative sentences.

Crisp, Informative Sentences

Crisp, precise sentences focused on providing information form the fourth factor contributing to the book's cohesion. Such sentences have an effect of remaining in the background while a reader absorbs information. Gornick sums up such writing: "keep the narrating self subordinated to the idea in hand" (10). The dutiful nonfiction writer does not seek undue attention and presents the reader with a work that is carefully crafted. Gornick attributes such skillful crafting to a writer's mental immersion in his or her setting, which we may also call good journalistic work: "It was the act of imagining herself as she had once been that enriched her syntax and extended not only her images but the coherent flow of association" (5). As a journalist, Sheean observed, talked, travelled, read, took notes, thought, and perhaps also remembered well. In the book, Sheean does not discuss his writing (except to mention, as we have seen, his desire to become a better writer). But from the book one gets a sense of a demanding writer, who wrote his observations exactly, who ensured he had the material for writing, and who thought about the material, connecting points and ideas.

Even granting that Sheean's book is based on his reporting and parts of it, the book acknowledges, were published in the *Atlantic*, the level of detail in the book and its careful organization show a writer who has high standards. Historian Deborah Cohen gives a few interesting details surrounding the book. In a letter to an English friend, Sheean wrote that he wanted the book to "make money" (Cohen 207). Sheean "had been paying attention to what sold" (207). The idea to write a memoir was suggested to Sheean by Harold Nicolson, a British politician, who was engaged in writing his own (207-208). Because his novels (there were three prior to *Personal History*, according to Johnson) up to that point had not been very successful, Sheean might have decided to take Nicolson's suggestion and write a novelistic memoir (Cohen 208). This tidbit suggests that Sheean must have put extraordinary efforts into *Personal History*. Literary critic Malcolm Cowley describes the book's writing in this way: "He [Sheean] has a clean narrative style, a sharp eye for color and incident, and at the same time a fair intellectual grasp of the forces operating beneath the surface" (50). *Personal History* is not just full of details and characters, but it makes good arguments and is expertly written—a model of writing.

The sentences in the book provide details—the book brims with information—but they also present reflection, evaluation, and humor; use irony, sarcasm, similes, and metaphors; and include numerous expressions in foreign languages, mainly French, Italian, and Spanish. Pondering the distance he had traveled since his university days, from Illinois to Bloomsbury, London, Sheean concludes that "the mind…has no geography" (*Personal History* 317). Sitting inside the Dome of the Rock in Jerusalem, Sheean sees the strange disconnect between its beautiful architecture and "religious hatreds that clustered round them" (346). In China, Sheean observes the irony of missionaries coexisting with "a murderous bombardment from the loving Christian navies" (201). As has been noted before, when his employer asks him for Rif-like stories, Sheean observes with ironic humor that good Chinese people "forestalled" his "effort to have personal adventures" (248). Traveling from China to Russia, Sheean compares Manchuria to a "dusty carpet" (258). Such sentences present a narrator with a distinct voice—observant, thoughtful, honest, exact, charitable—an effect that adds to the book's cohesiveness. The narrator's presence and its role in the book's cohesion are discussed next.

The Narrator's Presence

Vivian Gornick calls the presence of a narrator in a memoir "nonfiction persona" (26), a cultivated and detached perspective on one's material that helps a writer craft an effective story (12). Gornick also characterizes this presence as a "truth-speaking personae" (24). Explaining the implications of this presence for readers, Gornick states, "[It is] that organic wholeness of being in a narrator that the reader experiences as reliable; the one we can trust will take us on a journey, make the piece arrive, bring us out into a clearing where the sense of things is larger than it was before" (24).

Gornick mentions a medical student who eulogized a mentor after her death (3). The student composed her speech based on her apprenticeship experience with the mentor. The speech was cohesive despite different experiences it included because the speaker "imposed an order," her own. Gornick observes that "the better the speaker imagined herself, the more vividly she brought the dead doctor to life. It was, after all, a baptism by fire that was being described." In *Personal History*, Sheean does something similar (Gornick's phrase "baptism by fire" made me think of Sheean of *Personal History*). Sheean imposes his order—his imprint—on varied narratives in the book. Readers associate each narrative with Sheean, who provides a common link. This careful persona helps integrate the book's varied narratives.

Noted literary theorist F. K. Stanzel describes the presence of a narrator in an autobiographical piece in this way: "The first-person narrator is 'embodied' in the world of the characters" (90). In *Personal History*, Sheean is "embodied" and a character. His presence provides unity to the narratives in the book; in other words, readers associate them with the narrator. In every chapter, Sheean as the narrator is never far from readers' consciousness. Indeed, a powerful presence of a narrator may impart cohesion to dissimilar narratives because the reader might wonder what the narrator would do next or what would happen to him as a story expands. Sheean achieves such a presence not by overwhelming readers with personal tidbits or drawing attention to himself, but by scrupulous focus on information, the context underlying the information, views of leaders, concerns of people, and so on. In this way, by keeping narratives even, similar in size, shape, and voice, the presence of the narrator contributes to *Personal History*'s exemplary cohesion.

It should be noted that, in addition to its role in achieving a narrator's presence, the authorial first-person singular pronoun performs routine work of informing readers about the narrator's activities, thinking, or experiences. Thus, the combination of stories and Sheean's narrative persona contributes to the cohesion of various narratives in *Personal History*.

Conclusion

Personal History "would sell more than two million copies" (Cott 206). Evaluating the book and its author, journalism scholar John Maxwell Hamilton remarks, "What elevated Sheean even among luminaries in journalism was the literary quality of his reporting, his uncanny ability to situate himself in the slipstream of monumental news, and the intensity of feeling with which he viewed those events. All of that is on display in *Personal History* ("Vincent Sheean's" 125). According to Ronald Weber, the book was both "hugely popular" and "drew wide critical approval" (*News of Paris* 166). Calling the book "a sensation," Deborah Cohen mentions that "the Literary Guild chose it as the book of the month" (208). In his 1935 review, Malcolm Cowley calls the book "a work of art," suggesting that the book "contains the outline of a tragedy" (50). Mary McCarthy, who praised the book as "a first-class literary work," credits Sheean with "a warm, intuitive appreciation of human beings and a strong moral sense" (284).

Personal History is literary because of its cohesion, stories, and fine prose. Sheean would go on to write more memoirs, interweaving his narrating self with consequential world events. *Personal History* provided him with a form that came to define him. Johnson notes Sheean's persistent wish to become a successful novelist (333, 464). Although Sheean wrote several novels and some of them were successful, no book of his surpassed *Personal History* in popular appeal and critical acclaim (Johnson 728-730; Montgomery 32).

Chapter 3
Journalism, Writing, and a Passion for People

Continuing to explore literary journalism of Vincent Sheean as a foreign reporter, in this chapter, I analyze his book *Not Peace but a Sword*, which was published in 1939. The new memoir, a successor to *Personal History*, shows that the largely personal historian is in the past. Sheean seems to have become a journalist who writes about world events in ways that matter to people; the book focuses on ordinary people and refers to them in its last paragraph. Sheean has also become more essayistic and discursive. In his history of literary journalism, Hartsock characterizes the form as mainly narrative, but he mentions "discursive literary journalism" (*A History* 138), which includes reflection, exposition, and argument (136-138). In a more recent book, Hartsock advises critics to consider literary journalism as being along a "continuum" between two "extremes" of dry, objective reporting and "a solipsistic subjectivity" (*Literary Journalism* 3). *Not Peace but a Sword* falls comfortably nearer the narrative side.

Recounting a whirlwind of journalistic activity from spring 1938 to spring 1939, *Not Peace but a Sword* begins harmlessly enough, although Sheean hints at what is to follow. Sheean experiences a ride on the famous "Thirteen Bus" in London (Sheean, *Not Peace* 2). The bus meanders through landmarks and spectacles around celebrated and stolid streets. Looking out the window, Sheean finds that people of London are busy in their normal lives, apparently oblivious to events underway on the continent. In chapter two, the book shifts to the war between the Spanish republicans and nationalists (or fascists) around the river Ebro. The third chapter has Sheean visit a conference in Evian, France, on the issue of Jewish refugees. The chapter goes on to describe the persecution of Jews by Nazis in Austria and Germany. Next, Sheean returns to Spain to tell the story of people of Madrid and their resistance to the fascists. In addition, the book narrates and describes events in Czechoslovakia before and after the Munich Pact, a personal story about an American volunteer who fought and died in the Spanish civil war, and a quick but mostly futile visit to Spain, where the republican fight is over.

Did timeliness of the book (what rhetoricians call *kairos*), appearing when fascism threatened the peace of Europe and the world, have something to do with the focus on people and the book's more substantial discursive writing?

Writer and critic Louis Kronenberger, a contemporary reviewer, remarks, "Mr. Sheean roved during a year of almost unparalleled history-making, a year with all the movement and meaning of an epoch.…Not since the upsurge of European nationalism has one idea altered the map of Europe as Fascism did between March, 1938, and March, 1939" (58). Kronenberger adds that the happenings recounted in the book are "what every well-informed person knows already" (58). R. L. Duffus, another reviewer of the book, expresses an unusual hope that the "strong throb of a spirit" in the book's "writing" may help "check the rise of fascism" (16). James Gray, scholar of English, praises the book in these words: "Sheean, who had put himself honorably in the forefront of the fight to awaken the world to its danger [the rise of dictators], added a grim final word before the battle in *Not Peace but a Sword*" (131). An heir in form to *Personal History*, the book seems to have been well received.

Faced with grim realities experienced by ordinary citizens across Europe, it is not surprising that Sheean chose to focus on common people. For example, Sheean ends the chapter on Madrid with the following sentence: "In this one place, if nowhere else, the dignity of the common man had stood firm against the world" (*Not Peace* 199). The extent of discursive writing may be due to cataclysmic disturbances Sheean witnessed. As a foreign reporter, he perhaps felt compelled to explain disparate political forces and their changing circumstances.

As a writer, since *Personal History*, Sheean seems to have grown in confidence. He does not hesitate to give reasoned opinions and judge leaders or countries in *Not Peace but a Sword*. His understanding of the world affairs is rational—though not devoid of sentiments—and bluntly delivered. In a review after the publication, Charles Poore offers this evaluation of the book: "nothing he [Sheean] has written since 'Personal History' can equal it in force and clarity: and in maturity it excels the earlier testament that helped to shape the thinking of a whole American generation" (L 15). Lauding the book, journalist Kenneth Stewart writes that Sheean "spoke for many of us" in siding with "the common man" against "the dominant reality in Europe" (214). Reviewing the book in *The New York Times*, R. L. Duffus defends Sheean "for the sharp definitions in the picture he draws": "any reader will understand that Mr. Sheean had seen things which tested his calmness of judgment" ("A New Book" 1).

In referring to discursive writing in the book, I do not wish to provide an impression that the book is mostly expository, argumentative, or reflective. On the contrary, the book is mainly based on narratives. It includes scenes and stories that enable one to catch a glimpse of the time, places, and characters. Noting the book's "vivid scenes and stories" (59), Kronenberger praises Sheean for "creating a vigorous and graphic picture with himself in the foreground but not dominating it" (58). Kronenberger refers to the presence of a strong but restrained narrator in Sheean's prose. He admired the book "for its visual and personal qualities, its on-the-spot detail." Another contemporary reviewer, journalist Franz Hoellering, points to the "genre of [Sheean's] great success—reporting in a literary style," calling Sheean "a master" of the form (128). Duffus, who considered the book better than *Personal History*, writes that Sheean "has achieved a mastery that makes literature of the horror and indignation which swept over him with much of what he saw, the admiration for human courage that some other spectacles inspired in him" (1). Cott notes that the book's "eloquence compelled reviewers, and it sold well" (248).

The following aspects of *Not Peace but a Sword* make a good case to consider it as a work of literary journalism: a widely-praised story and a few stimulating scenes; the book's spartan language, reminding one of Lounsberry's phrase "fine writing" (*The Art of Fact* xv); and descriptions and "status details" (Wolfe 32). In what follows, I analyze these aspects of the book.

The Story of Jim Lardner

Many reviewers of *Not Peace but a Sword* praised the book's story of an American young man named Jim Lardner, who enlisted in the International Brigades of the Spanish republican forces. In his review, Charles Poore calls it the book's "best chapter" (L 15). R. L. Duffus ends his review with a reference to the story. Franz Hoellering notes the story's "unmelodramatic simplicity which is immensely effective." Louis Kronenberger also mentions the story. The story is told in a chapter called "The Last Volunteer" (Sheean, *Not Peace* 235).

Jim Lardner, son of American journalist and writer Ring Lardner, was a reporter who worked for the Paris edition of New York *Herald-Tribune* (236). He joined Sheean and Ernest Hemingway on a train to Barcelona, Spain, on March 31, 1938 (235). The three men wanted to see the state of the war after the recent reverses faced by the republicans (235-236). Both Sheean and Lardner were attached to the *Herald-Tribune* (236). However, Sheean was considerably more experienced as a reporter compared to the 23-year-old Lardner (243, 237). From Barcelona, Lardner went to a front of the war and, after returning, wrote a detailed story for his newspaper (242). When the story was published, however, it was substantially cut (243). In contrast, a piece by Sheean was published almost as it was written and placed in a conspicuous spot. Sheean proposed to Lardner that they discuss an arrangement that would ensure that both their stories are treated well by their employer. However, Lardner refused Sheean's help, asking him to continue his work.

After this episode, Lardner became quieter and more thoughtful (Sheean, *Not Peace* 244). One day, Lardner told Sheean that he would like to join the International Brigades, an army of foreign volunteers fighting for the Spanish republic. Surprised at this idea because the war seemed to be nearly over, the work of the foreign fighting force not going to be needed much longer, Sheean tried to dissuade the young man, especially since Lardner did not have any military experience (244-247). Hemingway offered Jim Lardner similar advice (247). However, Lardner pursued the goal of joining the International Brigades (248-249). He succeeded and was assigned, at first, to an inactive unit that gathered the misfits of the army (250). Lardner got himself out of this unit and managed to be assigned to the Lincoln Battalion, an American fighting force of the International Brigades (252-253). Sheean tells us that Lardner was the last American volunteer to join the International Brigades (266). Just when the Lincoln Battalion's war participation was approaching its end, Lardner went on a nightly mission and was killed (265-266).

Story consultant Kendall Haven distinguishes stories from other narratives and modes based on the following four criteria: "characters," "goals," "conflicts," and "struggles" (11, 20-26). According to Haven, characters are "central" to stories, which after all "happen to characters" (12); "no other [story] element has meaning and relevance without a character." Characters are willing to face conflicts and undergo struggles to accomplish a goal that they desire (12). Conflicts comprise "internal flaws and external problems [Haven combines these two in the word "obstacles"]...and the risk and danger associated with each [that is, with flaws and problems]" (12, 23). Struggles are characters' actions and reactions "to overcome conflict" (12, 25-26). Struggles thus pit characters against "danger[s]" and "risk[s]" (24, 81). An additional, secondary story element is a "crucible," "a conditional threat" (25), which can be described as something a character cannot lose (e.g., "time," in case of a threatened deadline, "pride," "love," and the like) (25).

Haven's story criteria may help us better appreciate Lardner's story because they emphasize characters. In Sheean's rendering of the story, Jim Lardner, the main character, looms large. In his questions to assess a story's effectiveness, Haven asks the following question about the element of characters: "Is the main character compelling and interesting?" (80). That several contemporary reviewers of Sheean's book noted Jim Lardner's story suggests an answer to this question. Other characters, such as Sheean himself, the newspaper for which both Lardner and Sheean wrote, or the idle unit that Lardner is sent to at first, add to the story's "obstacles and conflict [that are] sufficiently compelling" (80). Obstacles also arise from the main character's own background or situation (23). As stated before, Haven divides the term "obstacles" into "problems" and "flaws." While problems come from a character's environment, flaws are present within a character. The following is an analysis of Jim Lardner's story based on Haven's story criteria.

Character

Just before joining the International Brigades, Jim Lardner explains his decision in a letter to his mother in these words: "My closest friend and principal adviser here has been Vincent (Jimmy) Sheean, who told me not to join, which shows you how stubborn I am, if you didn't know" (Nelson and Hendricks 44). Referring to Catalonia and describing its appearance on the map, Lardner jokes that, although the region looks like a small country "about to be pushed into the Mediterranean," this land will never "be conquered" because "there are too many people here who are fighting for things they believe in, and too few on the other side" (44-45). He then lists 15 reasons why he decided to join the foreign fighting force. Among his reasons are a desire to "exterminate" fascism, "impress various people," "find material for some writing," learn about fear and danger, and "get in good physical condition" (45). Lardner then provides a few reasons against his decision, among them a possibility of getting killed and being a reason for his mother's "worry" (45-46). He tells her, however, that he has made up his mind, assuring her that he "hate[s] violence" and will not volunteer in any future wars should he survive this one (46).

As we see, Lardner's own words confirm Sheean's description of him as "stubborn" (Sheean, *Not Peace* 245). From the letter, Lardner appears to be straightforward, thoughtful, determined, idealistic, and a bit naïve (hardly a surprise for a twenty-three-year-old). Lardner's letter is dated May 3, 1938 (Nelson and Hendricks 44). Let's put Jim Lardner's joining the International Brigades in a larger context. In February and March 1938, the fascist forces had forced the republicans into "big retreats" (Bessie 384). It is true that the republicans launched an offensive in July, but they "never recovered from the defeat at Teruel [in February 1938]" (Kitchen 256-257). Barcelona fell to the fascists in January 1939 and Madrid in March (Bessie 385; Kitchen 258). However, in May 1938, with the war still going on, it might have been difficult for an idealistic young man to foresee the strength of the other side and anticipate which way the war might turn, especially as the alternative to the republican side was an anathema to him.

Sheean, who depicts Lardner in a neutral but precise manner, is generous toward Lardner's perspective to join the International Brigades: "I had to admit that if I had been his age, and thought as he did, and had the nerve, I would have done likewise" (*Not Peace* 246). As to Sheean's disinterested depiction of Lardner, Sheean mentions early in the story that in persuading Lardner he and Hemingway did not "attach an exaggerated value to Lardner's life in a war which had already cost more than a million lives" (248). Lardner's sketch by Sheean also reminds one of his light yet interesting early conversations with Rayna Prohme (Sheean, *Personal History* 217). Sheean refers to the list of reasons Lardner has prepared to convince himself, and others he considers important, of his decision (Sheean and Lardner's mother, for example) (*Not Peace* 246). However, Sheean does not go into the specifics of the list, summarizing the contents briskly. He also concedes that a military experience may have benefits for a young man (246). Nevertheless, as Lardner pointed out in his letter to his mother, Sheean tries to convince him not to go ahead with his decision to join the International Brigades.

Haven writes that a character needs to be developed based on several "layers," including "the first impression, sensory image, personality, activity," and "history" (21-29). The story of Jim Lardner includes all of these aspects. Sheean introduces Lardner, tells the reader what he looked like, and what his mannerisms were (his easygoing enjoyment of humor, for example). Sheean calls him "a pleasant-looking youth" with "brown hair," "long legs," "slight awkwardness," and "not particularly robust" (*Not Peace* 237). Sheean refers to his weak eyesight (needing glasses) (247), good manners (254), his general cheerful disposition (237), his obstinacy (which has already been mentioned), his job as a reporter, his knowledge about Spain (237), and his distinguished education (Harvard) (254). Also frequent in the story are references to Lardner needing a bath, an accidental occurrence because Lardner's hotel room in Barcelona lacked a bathroom, and he had to request Sheean to use his bathroom (242). Lardner also seems to have had a strong sense of humor, as seen in his reaction to a funny exchange between Sheean and Hemingway during their train journey to the Spanish border (237-238).

Overall, from Sheean's sketch, Jim Lardner comes across as an idealistic young man with good education and background. He also had some physical limitations. But his strongest qualities seem to have been his will and determination (which ironically might also have been his undoing in the end).

Goals

According to Sheean, Lardner wanted to join the International Brigades to fight fascism (*Not Peace* 258), which is also the top reason in Lardner's letter to his mother (Nelson and Hendricks 45). In addition, Sheean believed that Lardner also needed to prove to himself (and possibly to others) that he could face the fears and dangers of fighting in a war (*Not Peace* 258). In his letter to his mother, Lardner writes, adding as a thirteenth reason for his decision to join the International Brigades, "Because I want to know what it is like to be afraid of something and I want to see how other people react to danger" (Nelson and Hendricks 45). Sheean summarizes Lardner's list of reasons, but in the letter to his mother, Lardner includes all fifteen reasons.

Among the fifteen reasons, Lardner considers these four as the main motivators: his struggle against fascism, a potential impact of his decision on the official

American approach to the war, the necessity to have some firsthand experience of war in a time of war (the world had seen a World War a few years ago and—probably not fully appreciated by Lardner—was on the precipice of another), and a reference to a "girl in Paris," perhaps a desire to show her something (Nelson and Hendricks 45). I will return to the goals at the end of this analysis to show how Lardner reached two of his goals—which both he, in his letter, and Sheean, in his story, mention—to fight against fascism and to know that he could face the fears of fighting in a war; but the goals cost him his life.

Conflict

According to Haven, conflict in stories involve external problems and intrinsic flaws that characters confront, which presents challenges and constraints to them in pursuing their goals successfully. Conflict—that is, problems and flaws—also involves dangers (the extent of threats) and risks (probability of threats) (23-24).

Lardner was a foreign reporter in Paris, working for the New York *Herald-Tribune*, the newspaper for which Sheean also wrote (Sheean, *Not Peace* 236, 245). As has been stated, his initial work from Spain seemed to have received a lukewarm response from the newspaper. Both Lardner and Sheean saw this development as a problem or a threat. Sheean observes how good parts of Lardner's story seemed to have been cut (243). He also mentions Lardner's disappointment. Sheean offered to help Lardner to come up with a strategy that might result in a better reception of Lardner's work by his employer. However, Lardner refused any assistance in the matter. He also became a bit aloof from the profession of journalism and eventually turned to the International Brigades.

It is clear from these circumstances that the problem Lardner faced—his disappointing debut as a war reporter—was further complicated by his personal flaws, as seen, for example, in his rejection of Sheean's offer to help. Sheean was a much more experienced reporter and could have helped Lardner (indeed, Sheean wanted to). Moreover, because his story found a cool reception, Lardner seemed to have lost interest in the profession of journalism itself (245). This lack of interest might have been temporary, but it did seem to be strong enough for him to want to become a soldier. Such a reaction to an early professional disappointment shows a young man who is a bit too sensitive or one who craves quick success—both potential flaws.

Lardner also encountered problems in his desire to be part of the international fighting force in Spain. First, he tried to join at a time when the foreign fighters were expected to be withdrawn from the war (Sheean, *Not Peace* 244). Second, both Sheean and Hemingway tried to dissuade Lardner. Other journalists also tried to get him to change his mind (248). Such pressure from trusted mentors and peers is often a problem for a character. Once the International Brigades accepted Lardner, he was at first sent to what was a dysfunctional group. This development was perceived by Lardner as an outcome that would prevent him from his goal, that of participating in the Spanish republic's war against fascism (251). Lardner was subsequently able to convince officials of the Lincoln Battalion, an American fighting force in the International Brigades, to let him join (253). Later, while fighting the war with the Lincoln Battalion, Lardner was injured due to a bomb (261-262). He spent a few weeks in a hospital (262). His injuries were serious enough to earn him a longer reprieve from the war, but, once again, Lardner's obduracy prevailed, and he managed to join his battalion again (262). Lardner wrote about his injury to his mother, describing the incident and expressing hope that he would return soon (Nelson and Hendricks 400-401).

In addition to external problems, Lardner had some personal flaws or limitations, which acted as obstacles in the pursuit of his goals. We saw some of these flaws earlier (e.g., his refusal to accept Sheean's help). In addition, he had a weak eyesight (Sheean, *Not Peace* 247) and lacked knowledge of or training in weapons (250). An important flaw in Lardner can be described as his pride, a characteristic we will return to when discussing goals. As we saw, because his story from Spain did not receive the recognition that he felt it deserved, he seemed to have soured on his profession of journalism (243). However, one sees from his letter to his mother that he had not rejected his love of writing (Nelson and Hendricks 45).

Obstinacy was another flaw of Lardner that probably had a profound effect on his life. We saw how he refused any help from his more experienced journalistic colleague, Sheean. Later, when Lardner mentioned his desire to join the International Brigades, Sheean advised him to continue working as a journalist (Sheean, *Not Peace* 244), a suggestion Lardner dismissed. If fighting fascism was his goal, writing as a journalist was another way to pursue it, as Sheean himself had been doing. Lardner pointed out to Sheean that too many journalists were already employed in this work (245). Working as a journalist also requires courage in covering wars and conflicts. Thus the role of a journalist may also have addressed Lardner's need to prove to himself that he was courageous.

Conflicts often give rise to dangers (extent of threats) and risks (likelihood of threats) (Haven 24). The goal of fighting fascism by serving in the International Brigades posed a clear danger of death or severe injury. Lardner understood these possibilities, as seen from his letter to his mother (Nelson and Hendricks 46), and hinted at in Sheean's story (Sheean, *Not Peace* 247). Unfortunately for Lardner, the worst danger came to pass (266). Lardner's struggle to achieve his goals, fighting against fascism and conquering his fears, in the face of many obstacles—with their potential risks and dangers—was a testament to his determination (and, conversely, tragic evidence of his flaws such as pride and obstinacy).

Struggles

Struggles involve "actions" and "reactions" (Haven 25-26). Actions are efforts made by a character to achieve his or her goal (25). Reactions are "unconscious, automatic movements" when "something happens" and "a form of reflex action" (26). Lardner's initial struggle involved a reaction to the treatment his news story from Spain received. His sullen and introspective reaction lasts a few days and ends with an idea he then pursues. Throughout the story of Jim Lardner, he acts to achieve his goals. From talking to Sheean and Hemingway about his plans to join the International Brigades, to meeting the officials of the fighting force, Lardner pursues his goals (Sheean, *Not Peace* 244-249). His journalistic colleagues attempt to change his mind, but Lardner does not relent.

Once he finds out at Badalona that he has been assigned to an inactive unit, Lardner leaves, meets with the International Brigades officials again, and convinces them to accept him into the Lincoln Battalion. In his war memoir, Alvah Bessie, an American who served in the Lincoln Battalion when Lardner joined it, recalls George Watt, the battalion commissar, praise Jim Lardner as a "fine squad-leader, one of the best men" (325). Watt disagrees with Bessie that Lardner is a "good writer," saying that "he's learning things now that will mature him, make him a good writer." Bessie wanted Lardner to assist him with his bulletin preparation (322), a request that was denied. Sheean, who visited Lardner in June, noted that he seemed to be happy (*Not Peace* 257).

Jim Lardner was an active member of the battalion (260). He was pursuing his goal of fighting Fascism, and he also seems to have improved in courage. In fact, when he was injured in August, he was eager to get back to the battalion (262). In one of his last letters to his mother, Lardner writes about a "trench" he and a few other men dug to keep them safe from "the Fascist lines" (Nelson and Hendricks 413). Lardner pithily declares, "I never was so well paid for hard labor as by that feeling of comparative safety." Four days after the date of the letter, Jim Lardner was killed during a night operation (Sheean, *Not Peace* 265).

Goals

Although Jim Lardner died in his attempt to fight fascism and his greatest fears, Sheean's story suggests that he accomplished his goals. In his memoir, Alvah Bessie notes briefly, "We heard that Jim Lardner, on patrol the night before, had been killed or captured when his squad met sudden and unexpected fire" (341). Sheean is a little more detailed. He writes that Lardner and his men came up to a rising and heard some chatter. Lardner volunteered to check who was behind it, was spotted, possibly confronted or questioned those responsible, and was shot and killed (*Not Peace* 265-266). Although Jim Lardner died, he did achieve his goal of fighting against fascism (at the cost of his life). If the story Sheean heard from the leading members of the battalion about Lardner's death is true, and there is no reason to doubt it is not, then it is clear that Lardner died facing the fears and dangers against which he was anxious to test himself, as Sheean points out (258) and as Lardner's letter to his mother dated May 3, 1938, suggests (Nelson and Hendricks 44-46). Lardner expressed a possibility in the letter that he might be killed in the war. So it seems clear that he was aware of the dangers he faced but faced them regardless of the consequences.

Conversely, one may argue that Jim Lardner did not have to die to fight against fascism and to prove his courage to himself and to others for whom he cared (Sheean, *Not Peace* 270). As has been stated, he joined the International Brigades when their mission had nearly ended in Spain, something Sheean, Hemingway, and a few other journalists pointed out to Lardner to no avail. In his story, Sheean honors Lardner's willing sacrifice. However, it should be remembered that Sheean tried to dissuade Lardner from joining the International Brigades in the first place. Haven mentions another aspect of stories that he calls a "crucible" (25). This aspect refers to a motivator in pursuing one's goals that a character would not disregard, no matter what obstacles came in her or his way. For example, when a character is forced to abide by a deadline or face important consequences, the character often manages to persevere despite obstacles. Other crucibles may include qualities such as "pride," "loyalty," "love," and the like (Haven 25).

It may be argued with some basis that for Jim Lardner such a crucible was pride. He probably felt that he could not back down after confiding in so many people—Sheean, Hemingway, Lardner's mother, to name a few—his deep-rooted desire to fight fascism by enlisting in the International Brigades. Once he had declared his intention so emphatically, taking another course might have seemed to him to be susceptible to accusations of cowardice and similar other failings that his pride would not permit. Perhaps a stronger motivation for Lardner was his need to prove to himself that he could fight in a war, especially for his values, such as opposing fascism. Sheean has hinted at this possibility in his story (*Not Peace* 258). Therefore, it seems reasonable to say that pride played a role in Lardner's actions, with tragic consequences.

According to Norman Sims, one of the characteristics of literary journalism is "symbolism" ("The Literary Journalists" 4). Sheean refers to Stephen Crane's *The Red Badge of Courage* to discuss Jim Lardner. Like the soldier in Crane's book, Lardner had a compelling need to prove to himself that he could face the fears and dangers of fighting in a war (Sheean, *Not Peace* 258). Sheean also suggests that Lardner might have willingly given his life to help the cause of the

Spanish republic (270). He invokes Lardner's name in the plural ("Lardners of the world") to describe young volunteers of the International Brigades who risked or lost their lives to defend freedom and democracy (259-260). At the end of the story, Sheean sees a purpose in their sacrifices: "All those Lardners did not die for nothing. If the world has a future they have preserved it...for provinces and nations can be signed away, but youth and honor never" (270).

Three Stimulating Scenes

According to the *Oxford Dictionary of Literary Terms*, a scene depicts actions that occur at the same place and during a particular time (Baldick 323). Chris Baldick explains that a scene is detailed and shows actions "at roughly the same pace as that at which they are supposed to be occurring." Kendall Haven calls scenes "building blocks of a story" (84), stating that each scene is like "a ministory," which includes "conflict or struggle" and its resolution. Sue Hertz, an English scholar, describes scenes more broadly: "scene is the action, the setting, the characters moving, speaking, thinking, working, walking, feeling, plotting, observing. Scene provides the cinematic angle, bringing the reader in close to the subject and then expanding for a wider angle that encompasses more characters, more setting" (117).

Each of these characterizations of the term helps us understand this concept in its various manifestations. Some scenes are drawn out, occurring in one place and time (Baldick); some scenes combine disparate images (Hertz); and some scenes, like "mini stories," include a conflict and its resolution (Haven 84). Scenes involve action on the part of characters in a particular setting at a certain time; they engage readers, providing them with a better understanding of time, place, and people in a work.

All three scenes that I briefly analyze here occur in chapter four of the book, titled "Madrid" (Sheean, *Not Peace* 140). Together, they show a particular place and time, Spain in 1938, along with its people; the scenes also reveal Sheean's focus in the book on ordinary people. The chapter begins with Sheean in Valencia, southern Spain, visiting nearby "fronts" (141). Then, he boards a bus for Madrid (154).

The Bomb Shelter Scene

This scene occurs in a place called Castellón de la Plana in eastern Spain. The town had been a target of heavy bombing raids by the fascists (Sheean, *Not Peace* 144). It had good bomb shelters, which Sheean describes as "the best system of deep refuges in Spain," crediting them with saving people's lives. Although he had experienced bombing raids in other places, he had not visited any bomb shelter because either the raid was over swiftly, or he did not find any shelter (145).

At a hotel in Castellón de la Plana, Sheean got the last unoccupied room and had to share it with a Spanish officer from the Military Recruitment and Instruction Corps, who had traveled to the town along with Sheean (145). Sheean informs the reader that the officer went to take his dinner at a "mess" belonging to his military agency. When the officer returned to the hotel room, he found it difficult to locate his bed because of the darkness in the room, the lights having been turned out due to a bombing threat. He had to maneuver through clothes scattered on the floor and asked Sheean if they were his. Sheean said that they were. The officer then asked Sheean to keep his clothes on a chair next to his bed so that they did not obstruct movement in the event of a nightly alarm for a bombing raid. As their further exchange shows, what the officer did not say but implied was that they would need to go to a bomb shelter if there was an alarm.

What then ensued was a brief argument between Sheean and the officer. Sheean said that he believed that there was no safer place than others on such occasions. The officer sneeringly dismissed this idea and told Sheean that he must go to a shelter if there was an alarm (145-146). He praised the bomb shelters in the town and added that they were not far (146). However, Sheean continued to argue, which elicited a sharp rebuke from the officer. Just then, there was an alarm for a bombing raid. The effect of their exchange was such that Sheean at once rose, dressed quickly, and accompanied the officer to a nearby bomb shelter. On their way, the officer told Sheean that he should definitely visit a bomb shelter since he is also a journalist. Sheean found the shelter to be true to its reputation. It was spacious and safe, and the people who had assembled there seemed happy. There was no bombing raid, however, and on their way back, the officer seemed a bit "apologetic," explaining to Sheean that had there been a raid the shelter would have been an excellent refuge (147).

Although the dialogue between Sheean and the Spanish military officer is brief, it is entertaining, with the officer using—Sheean tells us—"the Spaniard's favorite oath" (145). The exchange between the men seems real, reminding a reader of similar incidents from their own lives, though not necessarily involving a bomb shelter. For example, it is common to find oneself sitting next to a stranger on an airplane. People also share apartments with others. Such occasions usually demand some consideration for views and comforts of those who are our temporary companions. There also occurs some give-and-take of opinions.

As a service member, the officer probably had more respect for a wartime routine and a better understanding of bomb shelters. It is touching to see him chastise Sheean, compelling him to go to the shelter, then explain to him why it was a good idea. The officer sticks in the reader's mind as a good Samaritan. It was not enough for him to look after himself by going to a shelter at the alarm. He needed to have Sheean there as well. The exchange tells the reader about Sheean, too, who was probably not too tactful. Sheean's statements in the dialogue seem flippant; for example, when he is asked about the clothes on the floor, he replies, "all over the place, I suppose" (145). The scene also shows us how people lived in this part of Spain during this time.

The scene has a quality of transporting us to a specific place and time. As readers, we can imagine the officer's peremptory manner, his punctilious habits, his prim appearance, his leaving the hotel in the morning to go to his work, his glance at Sheean who greets him later in the day, their brief exchange, before each begins to do something, probably sleep because of the forced darkness in the hotel room.

Management scholar Stephen Denning states that "when readers follow a story …they journey—virtually—with the storyteller into a different world. Implicitly the readers project themselves with the storyteller into a different mental location—the place where the story takes place—even though they have never physically left their static sitting position" (59). Haven calls scenes little stories (84), which can transport a reader or a listener to a time and place (Denning 59).

Two Arguing Strangers

This scene is made up almost entirely of dialogue. It takes place in Valencia, probably at Sheean's hotel or an establishment where he took meals (Sheean, *Not Peace* 148). There is little description of the setting in the scene except briefly at the end (154), and the scene could almost be read as fictional—it has a novelistic quality to it, two widely contrasting characters presenting their viewpoints. The characters may also be seen as composites, each representing a political ideology. However, a more likely possibility is that the dialogue was written based on Sheean's memory and perhaps some quick notes he took. When Sheean left the hotel, the two men were still arguing at the table where Sheean left them after he had finished his lunch (154).

The two Spanish men, one thinner and the other more robust, join Sheean at a table where he is eating (148-149). After observing how dissimilar they seem, Sheean decides to initiate a conversation between them, perhaps a journalistic technique to find out what common people think (149). So he asks them about the time when the last event took place at the bullring opposite the hotel. Sheean tells them that he remembers how church and bullfighting dominated towns in Spain several years ago when he was last in the country. Prompted by Sheean's remarks, the thin man states that the two institutions damaged the country, an opinion that starts the argument between the two men, with Sheean being a silent listener for the most part.

The more robust man concedes that there have been problems with the church in Spain. However, he objects to a wholesale rejection of it. At this point, Sheean includes a line in Spanish, spoken by the thin man, that lends authenticity to the scene. The line repeats his charge that there is nothing good about the church. The more robust man counters with a reference to the freedom of conscience, invoking the republic's thirteen-points program. The thin man, an anarchist, attacks the notion, saying that the church does not allow it and compels people to believe what it would like them to believe (149-150). The more robust man accepts some criticism of the church but sticks to his contention that the freedom of conscience is important in a democracy (150).

The two men then show their union identification documents. The thin man continues to speak in the same vein, acknowledging the other's freedom of speech but attacking the church just the same (150-151). Giving an example of his mother, a Basque Catholic, the more robust man asserts that no one should deny her right to practice her religion (151). The thin man responds that making an allowance for the church will only embolden it to interfere further in the country's affairs (152). His counterpart disagrees. Attacking the robust man's constant theme of the freedom of conscience, the thin man says that it is meaningless in the face of so much indoctrination by the church. Both men support the republic and want the fascists to be defeated (151), but they seem to have fundamentally divergent views about society and the country (150).

Historian Martin Kitchen refers to "persistent political jealousies, rivalries and even hatreds...between the CNT [an organization that represented the anarchists] and the communists" among reasons that weakened the republican cause (247-248). The scene just described appears to be an example of this conflict. There was a "militant" faction among anarchists, which resented communists, accusing them of amassing power (Kitchen 245). Conversely, "the communists consistently and vehemently denounced...anarchist experiments for disrupting production and distribution" (244). The thin man in the scene was an anarchist. The more robust man, whom Sheean did not think was either a communist or a socialist, was a member of a labor organization representing these ideological groupings (Sheean, *Not Peace* 150).

Save answer a question or two during their debate, Sheean did not engage with the men. Readers learn only a few details about them, such as their physical characteristics, mannerisms, and political and social beliefs. Later, in the chapter, Sheean provides a lengthy exposition of the political situation in Spain. He credits the Spanish communists with defending the republic against the fascists by broadening their appeal and securing important military assistance from the Soviet Union (Sheean, *Not Peace* 168-175). Kitchen agrees with this view: "The communists...became the party of moderation, normalcy, efficiency and a broad-based center-left coalition" (244). Both Sheean and Kitchen describe a divisive political situation in Spain with the republic on one side and many among the upper classes and members of the clergy on the other side (Kitchen 238, 242; Sheean, *Not Peace* 173). Some people among the republicans responded with violence (Kitchen 238, 243).

The thin man, despite all his denunciations of the church, probably represents a less "militant" anarchist (Kitchen 245). More extreme anarchists were opposed to find a common cause with the republican government. The more robust man seems to illustrate the official government line. At the end of the scene, when Sheean emerges from the hotel, he sees the bullring and thinks that the two men did not talk about it while arguing about its "one-time rival," the church (Sheean, *Not Peace* 154).

What is notable is that both men claimed to be on the side of the republic. Yet they vigorously argued about the role of the church, ignoring a more prominent threat of fascism. The more robust man could not relent from his theoretical debate over the freedom of conscience (which fascists would certainly violate when it suited them to do so), and the thin man had to condemn the church for all its past sins, knowing in all probabilities that the fascists would engage in their own indoctrination and curbs on various freedoms. Both men obsessed over the internal differences among the democratic forces while overlooking the threat to democracy itself. Thus, according to Kitchen, there was a "fundamental rift within the republican camp which seriously prejudiced their chances of defeating the nationalists [or the fascists]" (246).

The Bus Journey Scene

This scene involves a bus journey from Valencia to Madrid that Sheean undertook in May 1938 (Sheean, *Not Peace* 154). It took him "eleven hours and a half" to reach his destination (156). He felt cold throughout the journey, not having anticipated lower temperatures (155). There is not much dialogue in the scene, but there are a few interesting characters, and their actions make the bus journey scene stimulating. Sheean's seatmate is some sort of bureaucrat who is taking flowers for his fiancé in Madrid (155-156). Sheean tells us that the "paper wrapping" of the flowers came loose from time to time and a passenger offered to help (155). The bureaucrat—whom Sheean calls "my respectable friend"— kept the flowers "on his lap" and also below his seat (158, 155). Sheean mentions an "elderly woman...who became the recognized humorist of the bus" (156). She spoke the "rich, lusty language of the people." At one place in the journey, Sheean laughs at a conversation the woman is having with a man from whom she is trying to buy eggs (157). The conversation offends Sheean's "respectable" seatmate, who apologizes for the woman's language. But Sheean surprises him by saying that he enjoys the language of the woman.

Sheean twice mentions reactions of his seatmate in a sarcastic manner, the first time when the man tries to make a historical reference about a town, and, again, when he tries to engage Sheean in a conversation about the exchange rate. In the first case, Sheean wonders why the man made an odd historical comment when he could have mentioned other things about the town. The second situation occurs when Sheean asks a woman passenger about the availability of wine in Madrid (158). Joining the conversation, Sheean's seatmate refers to a strong dollar and asks Sheean about the exchange rate that he gets when he converts his money. Taking his question as a potential reference to the black market, Sheean replies that he exchanges his money through the official process. Despite his reply, according to Sheean, his seatmate continued to discuss the exchange rate (158-159). When they reach Madrid, Sheean notices that his seatmate is "pulling off" crushed petals from his flowers (160). However, Sheean asks his seatmate for directions to his hotel, who clearly explains how to get there. In addition, he loans Sheean a small coin—since Sheean has a big currency note—to buy a subway ticket. Sheean also praises the bus passengers for their affection toward Madrid, in particular, "a girl in a *mono*" (154-155, 159).

The scene of the bus journey is stimulating because it shows—partly through dialogue, partly through narration—power and magnetism of ordinary people. These people were no high officials or celebrities. They had simple concerns, going home. It is clear that Sheean enjoyed their company. The reader vicariously feels this enjoyment. The reader notices his admiration for the woman who told jokes, his irritation with his seatmate, his attraction to the girl wearing a *mono* (a type of "overalls") (155), and his goodwill toward his fellow passengers. Moreover, journeys are experiences with which most readers can identify. Journeys take us out of our concern with ourselves and make it easy for us to focus on others, on the world. Ordinary people acquire a liveliness during a journey that belies their nondescript lives.

Spartan Language

In his 1946 essay titled "Why I write," George Orwell states the following about his writing style: "I will only say that of late years I have tried to write less picturesquely and more exactly" (316). Orwell's quote describes Sheean's writing style in *Not Peace but a Sword*. In reading the book, one does not much notice the writing style, so absorbed is one in information that fills up the sentences. The panoramic quality of a memoir, seen in *Personal History*, has given way to a sparse essayistic style, which eschews verbal indulgence. The result is well-crafted prose. Yet the book displays a level of unselfconsciousness befitting a mature writer at the peak of his writing skills. According to R. L.

Duffus, the *New York Times* reviewer, the book is better than *Personal History* because Sheean "wrote it in a peculiarly selfless mood, distrusting words as a substitute for action" (1). Duffus adds that Sheean is "careful of his words" and..."writes with restraint."

Duffus's explanation for such a sparse style is that Sheean was deeply affected by what he witnessed, especially the sacrifice of those fighting for the Spanish republic. This reason may be true or at least partially responsible for Sheean's style. But one may also remember Sheean's words at the end of Personal History, ones that he imagined coming to him from Rayna Prohme. Writing accurately, precisely, was to be his aim. The aim is realized in *Not Peace but a Sword*.

Barbara Lounsberry uses the phrase "fine writing," borrowed from writer Annie Dillard, to refer to the writing of literary journalists (*The Art of Fact* xv). Among a few examples, Lounsberry mentions John McPhee's "plain prose for clarity." According to Dillard, plain prose "is honed to a bladelike edge" (215). She describes this prose style in the following way: "[plain prose] is as restricted and taut as the pace of lyric poetry....This prose has one supreme function, which is not to call attention to itself, but to refer to the world" (216). Calling plain prose "a means...not an end," Dillard states that this style can be used "to name the multiple aspects of experience one by one, with distance, and also with tenderness and respect." She calls the style "craftsmanlike" (217). Dillard's description of plain prose applies well to Sheean's prose in *Not Peace but a Sword*. The prose in the book informs and communicates as precisely as possible while avoiding expressive flourishes. The result is a polished prose, like planed timber.

Descriptions and Details

Vivid descriptions and concrete details characterize literary journalism (Hartsock *A History*; Connery "Discovering"). Kendall Haven defines description as a "discourse intended to give a mental image of something experienced" (40). Wolfe emphasizes paying attention to small details that distinguish people (32-33). These details invest characters with reality, depth, and power to engage readers (33). Descriptions and details in *Not Peace but a Sword* enable readers to imagine a scene or a character.

Here is how Sheean describes refugees in Spain: "They had weather-beaten faces, inured to suffering, and there was seldom a sign of emotion as they moved slowly onward from everything they had known in life to the uncertainties of a refugee camp in wartime" (Sheean, *Not Peace* 47). Another brief description of a battlefront hospital is evocative: "In the warm sunlight the nurses sat on the graveled driveway and rolled bandages" (67).

After the infamous Munich Pact, Sheean saw a speech by Adolf Hitler in Carlsbad, former Czechoslovakia (305). During the short speech, Sheean observes a dramatic detail: "one moment of the maniacal intensity...when he hit the balcony rail in front of him" before boasting that he "knew" he would speak here (313). Sheean's quick details about the Spanish communist leader Dolores Ibarruri, whose speech Sheean saw, point to a conflict in her personality: "There was a splendid earthy quality about her laugh, but her face was very sad in repose" (184).

Conclusion

Not Peace but a Sword is a fine book. It captures a critical year before the Second World War. Indeed, Sheean predicts the war (*Not Peace* 364). The Munich Pact seemed to him to be a guarantor of this outcome. The book intersperses narratives and discursive writing. In addition to the historical value of the book, it is notable for its well-crafted prose. If the Sheean of *Personal History* found a form for himself, in this book he took the form to a high point. Perhaps the most predominant theme in the book is Sheean's undisguised contempt for fascism. A close second theme is his admiration for the Spanish republic in its fight against its fascist enemies. The book mentions leaders. However, its focus is ordinary people. At the end of the book, he declares them to be more reliable than their leaders (367).

In the final chapter, Sheean makes a comment about journalism and writing, almost as if he were reminding himself of what these tasks mean (342). He juxtaposes these tasks because of how they had intermingled in his mind given the quick developments of the year. Specifically, he was concerned with the question of when to consider the book to be complete. Not facing Sheean's exact challenge, we can nevertheless assess the book in terms of journalism and writing—together, Sheean's lifework. If either task lacked in vigor, the book would have suffered. That it turned out to be "in solid style, a book" (Kronenberger 58) shows how well Sheean performed both tasks.

If literary journalism produces "a work of art" (Weber, *The Literature* 4), *Not Peace but a Sword* makes a good case for itself to be seen as a product of such a journalism. It is part history, part memoir, part narrative, and part discursive. It is a result of skilled journalism and masterful writing.

Chapter 4
Traces of a Time

Published in 1943, *Between the Thunder and the Sun* was Vincent Sheean's third memoir, after *Personal History* and *Not Peace but a Sword*. Before *Personal History*, Sheean had published *An American among the Riffi* (1926) and *The New Persia* (1927), two books based on his personal experiences, but these two books focused on specific parts or regions of the world. It was *Personal History* with its grand, global expanse that appears to have set a precedent for the two books that followed, as noted by the reviewers of *Not Peace but a Sword* (Hoellering 128) and *Between the Thunder and the Sun* (Thompson 4). Specifically, reviewing *Between the Thunder and the Sun*, Meribeth Cameron states, "This work continues the autobiographical narrative which the author began in *Personal history* and *Not peace but a sword*" (379). A brief review by the *Atlantic* also calls the book the "third installment of...*Personal History*" ("Review of" 127).

Between the Thunder and the Sun is vast and sweeping, covering enormous geographic territory, even if Sheean spent only a small amount of time in many places, especially in the Asia-Pacific, in what may be called stopover visits. The first chapter narrates and describes the time Sheean and his wife, Dinah, spent at the Salzburg Music Festival in Austria. The chapter then shifts to a seaside chateau in Cannes, France, owned by Dinah's aunt. The couple made multiple visits to both the festival and the vacation home in Cannes between 1935 and 1939. In chapter two, Sheean tells the reader about Italy and France in 1940, when France was invaded and occupied by Nazi Germany. The next two chapters find Sheean in Britain, where he witnessed the famous Battle of Britain (though he writes that he was not aware of the term when the battle was going on) and the bombing of London by the Luftwaffe. In subsequent chapters, Sheean writes about his lecture tour in the United States; an assignment aboard a Royal Navy ship and Germany's invasion of Russia; a visit to China via Australia, New Zealand, Indonesia, Singapore, and Burma; and a return to the United States via the Philippines and other Pacific islands. Something of the quality of this period, a world in turmoil, seems to have rubbed off on the book. The result is that the book leaves the reader with traces of this important period.

In his 1995 co-edited volume on literary journalism, Norman Sims recalls a comment on the form by a fellow scholar: "Professor Tom Connery of the University of St. Thomas remarked recently that literary journalism delivers 'this felt sense of the quality of life at a particular time and place,' and that it addresses a question cultural historians pose: 'How did it feel to live and act in a particular period of human history?'" ("The Art of Literary Journalism" 4). In *Between the Thunder and the Sun*, Sheean provides an answer to this broad, panoptic question.

Another quality of literary journalism that is prominent in the book is "interpretation," a widely recognized feature of the form (Wilson "Chapter 1"). Connery states that "a literary journalistic account did not just record and report, it interpreted as well" ("A Third Way" 6). Calling a reporter's "judgment" indispensable, former foreign correspondent Tom Fenton explains its role: "A foreign correspondent's utility can be boiled down to three practical functions: seeing the events, filtering the important parts down to news, and infusing a point of view where necessary. But all three gel into something greater than the sum of their parts when the correspondent's own judgment helps to shape the message" (199). Sheean evaluates actions of political leaders, discusses implications of events, and comments on people's responses to devastating changes happening around them. In fact, in a brief review of the book, Robert Gale Woolbert finds Sheean's "interpretations often illuminating."

In an essay titled "Being There," which refers to reporting immersed in a place, literary journalist Anne Hull argues that "it is very difficult to integrate news with writing" (42). She advises reporters to "pay attention to the sense of place," "go to church" (because "church is a good place to learn about community"), "use the language of the people you're trying to capture," and "be as open as you possibly can with your subjects" (42-43). In *Between the Thunder and the Sun*, Sheean has done all or most of these things. For example, in the scene of Sheean's meeting with former French prime minister M. Leon Blum, Sheean uses brief French expressions of Blum to convey his thoughts. Sheean also meets with old friends in an Italian lakeside village, who tell him that they oppose Italy's alliance with Germany (Sheean, *Between the Thunder* 98). Sheean communicates this sentiment in a radio broadcast to America. Although he is criticized for his report, Sheean informs the reader that later developments supported what he heard.

Hull's point about integrating news and writing deserves elaboration. It is true that journalists learn to write news reports—as Jack Hart modestly says of his early career (139)—but writing a comprehensive book connecting varied newsworthy events requires talent and skill. In his book about journalistic storytelling, Jack Hart confesses, "I've occasionally commiserated with disappointed reporters…while we pulled the plug on a story that took weeks of work" (146-147). R. Thomas Berner gives an example of a newspaper editor who said, "Too many of our stories mash facts together with no more structure than a tottering inverted pyramid" (x). Sue Hertz points to this challenge referring to nonfiction writers: "emerging writers feel often overwhelmed" (xiii). Praising

Sheean's reporting and writing, fellow journalist Kenneth Stewart states that Sheean "made events real," which helped in "a closer communication with the newspaper-reading public" (204). Stewart notes that not every journalist can be like Sheean: "If we all had the powers and penetration of the Sheeans...who would read the copy, write the headlines, put the paper together?" (326). In his review of *Between the Thunder and the Sun*, Craig Thompson praises Sheean for melding disparate episodes into a unified narrative with a "consistent viewpoint" (4).

Between the Thunder and the Sun also attracted criticism. Reviewing the book for *The Nation*, writer Louis Fischer finds fault with the book for "reporting a little conversation and a few externals" ("The Boy from Illinois" 566). Fischer takes Sheean to task for not "looking too closely" (567), wondering whether the ongoing war affected his judgment. Calling out Sheean's partial embrace of "British aristocracy," Fischer reminds Sheean that members of this group failed to help the Spanish republic. Fischer's advice to Sheean: judge people by their deeds, not "words." In Sheean's defense, it should be said that he criticizes the stance of the British "upper classes" toward the Spanish civil war (Sheean, *Between the Thunder* 78-79), scolding the "blindness and stupidity of the privileged order everywhere" (67). At the same time, Sheean had a few friends among these people (238). Hence, he appears to have moderated his criticism of their views and attitudes. Sheean pointed out that "the Tories" (Fischer, "The Boy from Illinois" 567) governed Britain at present and had dominated the British society and politics for generations (Sheean, *Between the Thunder* 243). Moreover, they were determined to defend Britain, unlike the politicians of France (242).

Hartsock states that literary journalism attempts to reduce the distance between an author's subjectivity and his or her subjects (or objects) of writing (*A History* 141). Reducing this gap requires immersion in a setting and use of concrete details. A vivid and "empathetic" depiction helps a reader understand a subject better and add details using imagination (142). Sheean's portrayal of a few privileged friends is lifelike. Sheean achieves this effect by providing concrete details based on close observations and interactions (despite Fischer's criticism of not "looking too closely," which refers to comparing deeds and words of Sheean's privileged friends). Thus, contrary to Fischer's critique, Sheean's effort engages readers and is literary journalism based on Hartsock's position. This point made, it is true, as Fischer notes, that the book skims through scenes and episodes, giving a feeling of agglomeration and accretion rather than world-building and storytelling found in his earlier two memoirs.

Even Sheean's accounts of the music festival in Austria or his visits to the seaside mansion of his wife's aunt—full of details as these engagements are—seem lightly sketched, giving a faint appearance of a world unlike a well-etched one, as was the case, for example, in his Rif journeys or his reporting from the Spanish war. The account of the fall of France contains imagery and interesting character insights (M. Leon Blum, for example). Yet, barring a few exceptions, the chapter only hints at a world that is facing an existential crisis. In addition, in what may be seen as limitations of this book as a work of literary journalism, the book contains more of historical narration, exposition, commentary, and reflection—fewer scenes or stories.

Despite its limitations as a work of literary journalism, the book contains aspects of the form, three of which I discuss in this chapter: "portraying character" (Fontaine & Glavin, Jr. 2), "imagery and symbolism" (Lounsberry, *Writing Creative* 122), and "personalized, subjective" writing (Applegate xvi).

Portraying Character

In *Between the Thunder and the Sun*, Sheean has drawn several characters that linger in a reader's mind. Three such portrayals are those of Aunt Maxine, the owner of the seaside chateau in Cannes, M. Léon Blum, former prime minister of France and a socialist leader, and Captain Charlie Todd, "A.D.C. to the Governor" of Guam, an American island in the Pacific. What binds these disparate characters is their depiction by Sheean based on his careful observation and interactions with them. Journalist Anne Hull advises literary journalists to "think like a photographer" and "watch" (40). Connery also mentions "memorable characters" or "richly developed characters" as an aspect of literary journalism ("Discovering" 33-34).

Aunt Maxine was Maxine Elliott (her adopted name; her real name was Jessie Dermot), a famous American stage actress in the "early 1900s" (Sheean, *Between the Thunder* 28; Young 6). Maxine, originally from Maine, was an aunt to Dinah, Sheean's wife (Sheean, *Between the Thunder* 28, 34). Dinah's father, Sir Johnston Forbes-Robertson, who was an English actor, had married Maxine's sister (Sheean, *Between the Thunder* 27, 168; Cott 208). Lewis C. Strang, a "drama critic" (Bordman and Hischak 592), describes Maxine's acting "style" as "light, airy, natural, never weighty and never blind" (328). He further characterizes Maxine as "charming with a constant suggestion of almost matronly dignity." Strang's attributes appear to fit qualities with which Sheean portrays Maxine in *Between the Thunder and the Sun*.

Aunt Maxine had "built herself a white palace" on the coast near Cannes and named it "Château de l'Horizon" (Sheean, *Between the Thunder* 28). Independent and confident, Maxine was sociable and liked to entertain distinguished guests and people from high society. For Sheean, Maxine "existed all at once...and you never thought of questioning her afterward." Sheean also refers to her "iron...ambition" (32). Maxine had little interest in "music or pictures [and]...read hardly anything" (37). But she had a good knack for managing money and knew a lot about her investments (36). Sheean heard praise about this ability of hers from a finance professional known both to him and Maxine.

Maxine was hospitable and always appreciated guests in her house, even if they displeased her in some way (30). Sheean's observation of her when they first met at her chateau shows her innate positivity and polished worldliness: "I was noticing above all her firm cordiality, as if the sudden marriage of a favorite niece to a total stranger was something she had long anticipated with pleasure" (29). One may suspect a bit of theatricality in Maxine's behavior—indeed, she was a stage actress, after all. But a stronger sense convinces a reader that Maxine really was this way, a positive person who liked to think highly of others unless shown wrong. Sheean describes Maxine's "childish...snobbishness" (32). His illustration of this quality again makes the reader see her as a unique individual, perhaps like someone the reader knows or knew. Sheaan illustrates this quality, "The kind of snobbishness that says, 'Of course a duke's much nicer than anybody else'" (32-33). Sheean writes that Maxine's aplomb made it difficult to think that she was from a small town in Maine and had been a stage actress (34). His point is that Maxine was not a born aristocrat but grew to be one in her manner and inclinations. Thus, despite sharing little with prime ministers and monarchs, she appeared entirely at home in their company. The book describes a dinner Maxine gave to the Duke and Duchess of Windsor, Edward VIII and his American wife, Wallis Simpson, attended also by Winston Churchill, Lloyd George, Vincent Sheean, and his wife.

Literary critic Edmund Wilson refers to Aunt Maxine in his praise for Vincent Sheean's ability to portray a character:

> What sets Mr. Sheean off from the ordinary writer of memoirs...is his ardent sense of human greatness. Nothing, for example, could be more different from the way in which celebrities are usually described than the way of Mr. Sheean in such a book as *Between the Thunder and the Sun*. In his account of a house-party on the Riviera, he can give you the colors and contours of Maxine Elliott and Winston Churchill—like a portrait painter in the best old tradition—in such a way as to make them impressive without relinquishing a strong sense of character and personal idiosyncrasy. (*The Shores* 744)

Sheean met with the French leader and former prime minister M. Léon Blum in his "comfortable apartment with windows over the Seine" (Sheean, *Between the Thunder* 126). Sheean begins by writing that he did not like Mr. Blum's politics, especially his "pacifism" (123). What Sheean means by this term is that nations need to engage in a conflict to defeat forces against democracy. However, Sheean liked the French leader's "ability to write and speak good French." Sheean continues his evaluation by telling the reader that Mr. Blum had lived in relative ease and comfort and showed "a sort of shrinking from fact" when faced with ugly realities of life, such as a war (124-125). He blames the French leader for not standing behind the Spanish republic and allowing it to be defeated by General Franco's forces (125). He believes that a democratic Spain would have been a source of strength for neighboring France against Fascist dictators.

At the start of his interview, Sheean observes that the French leader is "dressed" comfortably "in gray flannel pyjamas...of considerable elegance" (126). Sheean concludes that "this style of clothing...had given him the reputation of being extravagant." As they talk, Sheean discusses a conversation he had with Winston Churchill at Aunt Maxine's chateau (127). Churchill told Sheean about the qualities of a political leader. Sheean tells Mr. Blum that Churchill was not a capitalist. The French leader replies that Mr. Churchill did not have "the capitalist soul." Sheean was struck by the manner of Mr. Blum's response and notes that "it implied a whole series of kindred ideas."

Sheean tells the French leader that France and Britain will have Russia as a partner in the war against fascism (129). Mr. Blum disputes this idea, stating that "all the evidence is to the contrary." Mr. Blum then asks Sheean if he "[saw] any signs of...panic...among our people" (130). Interestingly, Mr. Blum accepts that Britain and France could have approached Russia before Germany did (129). But he asserts that it is too late now to depend on Russia (129-130). As we know from history, however, Germany invaded Russia, and it ended up joining Britain, France, and the United States. Historian Martin Kitchen attributes the reluctance of Britain and France to work with the Soviet Union to its perceived support of undemocratic practices in the Spanish republic (289). The reader sees in Mr. Blum an affable and genial politician, but one who is unable to imagine a different possibility.

On his return journey to the United States from China, Sheean traveled via a number of countries and islands in the Pacific region: Philippines, Guam, Wake Islands, and Midway Islands. At Guam, a marine officer named Captain Todd was waiting to take Sheean to the island's governor, Captain McMillin (Sheean, *Between the Thunder* 377-381). Captain Todd, probably in his late twenties, is also known as Charlie (381). He is both an assistant to the governor and the police chief for the island (379). On first seeing Captain Todd, Sheean notices the young man's "spotless white" uniform with a "gleaming gold...aiguillette" (377-378). Sheean is unkempt from the journey and feels a bit "ashamed" (377). Captain Todd drives Sheean through the island to the governor's mansion. He praises his job, the island, and his supervisor, the governor. He ensures that Sheean is comfortable at the hotel on the island and takes him to the "Officers' Club" (378-382). Sheean mentions that Captain Todd's hair got "tousled" by itself (384). Captain Todd talks to Sheean about his plans to return to the United States, and they agree on a date when they will meet in San Francisco (383).

Captain Todd quips that their plans depend on what the Japanese will do (384). It is late November 1941, and a few days later Japan attacked Pearl Harbor. Later in the chapter, Sheean makes an oblique reference to Charlie Todd, expressing a possibility that he might have been taken a prisoner by the Japanese (404). In fact, Japan invaded Guam after the attack on Pearl Harbor, and Charlie Todd is captured (Sood). He spent the next four years in Kobe, Japan (Sood).

Later in the book, in a slight reference, Sheean mentions Captain Todd's fate (*Between the Thunder* 404). The character of Captain Todd—a faraway soldier serving his motherland, doing his job well, and enjoying it—is one that will likely please many readers. When Captain Todd says goodbye to Sheean at his hotel ("Banzai!"), late at night, having taken care of the guest throughout the day (Sheean, *Between the Thunder* 384-385), one sees the goodness of the marine, his affection for someone from his home country who is visiting him on a remote, nondescript island. Of course, Sheean was not just anyone; he was a famous foreign correspondent.

Imagery and Symbolism

Chris Baldick, a scholar of English, differentiates between imagery and symbols: imagery refers to "those uses of language in a literary work that evoke sense-impressions by literal or figurative reference to perceptible or 'concrete' objects, scenes, actions, or states" (177); and symbols can be "anything that stands for or represents something else beyond it" (350). According to Ross Murfin and Supryia M. Ray, both scholars of English, imagery refers to "the language used to...represent any sensory experience" (238). The term also includes "figures of speech such as simile, personification, and metonymy." The authors describe a symbol as "something that...stands for or suggests something larger and more complex—often an idea or a range of interrelated ideas, attitudes, and practices" (504).

Sheean uses figures of speech, such as metaphor, metonymy, and synecdoche, to depict fretful behavior of privileged people he saw in Cannes. He criticizes them for overlooking the dangers of fascism. He refers to a "world-struggle" "writh[ing]" in front of them in the living room (metaphor) (*Between the Thunder* 78). He calls them "silken anxieties" (metonymy) and "the fashionable mind" (synecdoche).

Sheean paints a vivid picture of "the first major air assault on London" by drawing on imagery (September 7, 1940) (Deighton and Hastings 166). Author Len Deighton and journalist Max Hastings describe the nighttime bombing that Sheean witnessed: "From 8:10 pm until 4:30 the following morning, 318 bombers continued the attack in waves along nine miles of Thames waterfront; 448 civilians were killed in London and the suburbs, and many more badly injured" (169). Accompanied by American journalists Ed Murrow and Ben

Robertson, Sheean heard and saw the German planes (Sheean, *Between the Thunder* 220). They moved to a relatively safer spot, changing their location once more (221-223). They watched the attack until the early hours (226). In describing the fires because of the bombing, Sheean employs metaphoric phrases such as "a strange survey of damnation" and "a vision of the end of the world" (225). He conveys his feelings through a metonymic statement: "Here on a hilltop by the Thames we watched the centuries hurl themselves into the flames." He metaphorically portrays the inevitable German invasion of western Europe: "the gray rivers of the German flood…roll[ing] westward" (83).

Sheean uses symbolism effectively on at least two occasions. He narrates a scene at Aunt Maxine's chateau involving the former king of England, Edward VIII, his wife, Winston Churchill, and the former British prime minister Lloyd George (61). These dignitaries, along with Maxine, Sheean, and his wife, make up the dinner party. Sheean performs the role of the "host," supporting Maxine. The conversation turns to coal mines and "bathing" facilities at mine "pitheads" (64). The king and his wife, "the Duchess," praise German mines that they recently visited (63-64). Mr. Churchill is not pleased with the royal couple's talk (64). Churchill then mentions a piece of legislation that he had offered but it was rejected by the "miners' representatives" (64). The conversation then shifts to why the bill may have been rejected, with the king suggesting a theory that "the miners' wives" like "washing" their husbands (64-65). Sheean tells us that Maxine looked bored with the subject and that soon the women retired to another location (65-66). Summing up the scene, Sheean states that "to all at that table…the miner of whom they spoke was alien…to be tolerated…but not loved" (66). Thus, through the scene, Sheean shows the unfairness of the British (or any other) class system, one fostering inequality.

Another effective use of symbolism is found in Sheean's description of Notre Dame de Paris. Sheean and a fellow reporter are on the way to the American embassy when Sheean sees a crowd around the famous cathedral (Sheean, *Between the Thunder* 146). He wants to stop and inquire, but his colleague taunts him about his religiosity (falsely, as it turns out), and Sheean gives in and they continue to the embassy. At the embassy, Sheean's suspicion about something afoot at Notre Dame is confirmed. When they reach the cathedral, they observe official cars and see members of the French government leaving the church (147). The crowd that has assembled is observant but stoic (147-148). These people don't have any reaction seeing their soon-to-be-former political leaders (148). The German invasion is expected any day. Sheean reads in the people's reaction their desire to tap into the spirit of a bygone age when the great cathedral was built (149). He says that the French people have come to Notre Dame because they derive their strength from an age that made "France itself" (149-150). He sees in their congregating an urge to connect with their origins, to remind themselves of how far they have come as a people (152). In short, to Sheean, the French people's visit to Notre Dame at that moment was symbolic.

Personalized, Subjective Writing

Literary journalism is marked by "personalized" and "subjective" writing (Applegate xvi; Connery, "Discovering" 5; Connery, "A Third Way" 8; Boynton, xxi). This aspect is almost fundamental to literary journalism. Sheean's writing in this and other books is highly subjective. But in this memoir, perhaps more clearly than the earlier two, Sheean's subjectivity is unmistakable.

As it becomes evident that Germans have begun their invasion of France, Sheean and his colleagues ask for broadcasting time from "the American radio companies" (Sheean, *Between the Thunder* 141-144). However, their requests are denied because the companies do not want "un-neutral" information; they do not want to "disturb the public equanimity" (144). An exasperated Sheean writes in the book, "The theory…to the effect that the public needed only the facts in order to make up its own mind, was vitiated by…ways in which these facts were presented, as well as by the proved slowness of the mass to appreciate their significance" (144). In a book published nearly six decades after *Between the Thunder and the Sun*, former foreign correspondent Tom Fenton makes a similar point: "the public deserves to know what it doesn't want to know…yet" (205).

One of Sheean's colleagues to be denied radio time was Dorothy Thompson, who "in 1939…had 7.55 million readers in 196 newspapers, plus 5.5 million radio listeners on NBC" (Daly 233). Journalism scholar Christopher Daly states that "when Dorothy Thompson went on NBC on Monday evenings… Americans made a point of being near their radios" (219). Daly notes that in the early 1930s, "news on radio" had to avoid being "too partisan" (234). He adds that "news in the sense of original *reporting* had yet to come to radio" (emphasis in the original). In 1937, "Bill Paley of CBS" declared the mission of his company to be "wholly, honestly and militantly non-partisan." After the experience of propaganda mixing with news during the first world war, people in the news business—as well as the public—were "wary about claims of cruelty" (Daly 241).

In addition, a few prominent news media personalities, such as Colonel Robert R. McCormick and William Randolf Hearst, opposed America's "involvement" in the war (Daly 245). Daly quotes Hearst who denounced "Nazis, Communists, Fascists, imperialists" alike, accusing them all of "striving for power and territory" and "seeking…a new prize, a new victim." Moreover, as Michael Schudson, a scholar of journalism, notes, "Objectivity…by the 1930s, was an articulate professional value in journalism" (157). Schudson states that the notion of objectivity became important as a bulwark against doubt, "skepticism," given the recent intrusion of "propaganda" in news (122-144).

On the other hand, "interpretive reporting" also received more support during the 1930s (147-148). The American Society of Newspaper Editors accepted interpretation as a necessary quality in journalism (Schudson 147-148). Interpretation was seen as especially important to foreign reporters, "who felt the need for it most deeply" (147). Schudson quotes one such reporter, Raymond Gram Swing: "If European news is to be comprehensible at all it has to be explained. If it is explained it has to be explained subjectively. There is no getting around it, the man in Europe who is of most value to his newspaper is the man who expresses opinions in his writings" (147). Sheean offered his interpretation in his journalistic works.

Literary journalist Ted Conover explains the importance of personalized, subjective reporting and writing in these words:

> The point is that by simply spending time with people, being at their sides as they encounter challenging situations—by hanging out, in other words—you learn a lot about them than you might by only conducting interviews. By eating with them, traveling with them, breathing their air, you get more than just information. You gain shared experience. And often you get powerful true stories. (11)

Vincent Sheean followed these practices. He met with people, traveled, went to theaters and other artistic performances, observed people, talked to soldiers, met and talked to political leaders and other distinguished individuals, attended parties and gatherings, and visited city squares and other places of interest, among other activities.

Conclusion

Between the Thunder and the Sun reads more like a memoir than *Personal History* and *Not Peace but a Sword*. Although Sheean's focus, as usual, is on the world around him, Sheean as a narrator is a lot more visible in the book. The writing is clear, and, in places, striking and vivid. However, it lacks the polished prose found in *Not Peace but a Sword*. Prominent characteristics of literary journalism such as scenes and stories are not frequent in the book. Instead, the book moves through episodes and abounds in descriptions, exposition, and commentary. Nevertheless, the book has a few features of literary journalism. A few characters stand out for their lifelike portrayal. The book's use of imagery and symbolism is noteworthy. Lastly, perhaps because this book reads more like a traditional memoir, readers find a more explicit defense by Sheean of his subjectivity.

Chapter 5
A Personal Homage to Gandhi

In the summer of 1947, a strange thing happened in Vincent Sheean's life (Johnson; Sheean, *Lead, Kindly* 231). As a foreign correspondent, Sheean followed many of the world's events closely and perspicaciously. He had been following the events unfolding in India, which was on the verge of independence (Johnson; Sheean, *Lead, Kindly* 165). He was in Vermont, at the house of his friend Dorothy Thompson (Johnson; *Lead, Kindly* 231). He had a premonition that Mahatma Gandhi, India's principal leader, would be assassinated (Johnson 506; Sheean, *Lead, Kindly* 204). He also saw himself as trying to obstruct Gandhi's assassin (Johnson 506; Sheean, *Lead, Kindly* 177).

Sheean believed that Gandhi's noble life was near the point of its predictable, sacrificial end (Sheean, *Lead, Kindly* 176, 232). He shared his intuition about Gandhi with the editor of the *Holiday* magazine, who agreed to send Sheean to India (Johnson 508, 518; Sheean, *Lead, Kindly* 168-169, 176). Later, Sheean wrote an "article about Gandhi" for the magazine (Sheean, *Lead, Kindly* 228). Sheean also believed that Gandhi's life would be taken by a Hindu (176).

Premonitions were not uncommon occurrences for Sheean (Johnson 265). He was prone "to be present at history's turning points" (Montgomery). In his review of *Personal History*, Malcolm Cowley notes, "[Sheean] always had a nose for scenting out disasters and cataclysmic changes" (50). Edgar Snow, another American foreign correspondent who was in Delhi in January 1948, recalls hearing from Sheean about his premonition involving Gandhi: "It was his 'theophantic moment,' as Jimmy Sheean put it; the precise time had arrived for him to enter the pantheon" (398).

This chapter examines Sheean's *Lead, Kindly Light*, published in 1949. The book can perhaps best be seen as a personal homage to Gandhi. It contains seven chapters and four segments in an appendix. The chapters' topics can be summarized as follows: a preface (chapter 1), on Hinduism and Gandhi (chapter 2), Gandhi on *The Bhagavad Gita* (chapter 3), Gandhi's biography (chapter 4), Sheean's interviews with Gandhi and Gandhi's assassination (chapter 5), immersion of Gandhi's ashes in the confluence of the holy rivers in Allahabad (chapter 6), and Gandhi's contribution to the world (chapter 7). The first three segments in the appendix give additional information about Hinduism, Gandhi's interpretation of the *Bhagavad Gita*, and a few Hindu religious and social reformers who came before Gandhi; the last segment contains three Christian hymns that Gandhi liked. The book uses both narration and exposition (something that Sheean himself mentions) (Sheean, *Lead, Kindly* 4); specifically, along with the story of Sheean's journey to India and all that followed, the book includes historical narratives, description, commentary, and reflection.

Sheean also published a brief biography of Gandhi. He seems to have remembered Gandhi until the end of his life. In a December 1974 interview he gave to *The New York Times*, a few months before his death, Sheean stated: "Gandhi...had everything in the world to say and nothing to say it with. You could write yourself into a coma about Gandhi with ease" (Shenker 41).

Lead, Kindly Light may be considered in part a work of literary journalism. My claim is based on the following two aspects of the book: 1) the story of Sheean's journey to India during 1947-48, which includes his two interviews with Gandhi; his presence at Birla House, the temporary residence of Gandhi in Delhi where he was killed, at the time of his assassination; and his visit to Allahabad for the immersion of Gandhi's ashes. The assassination occurred in the garden of the residence. Gandhi used a part of the garden for his prayer meetings. Sheean did not see the assassination but heard the shots. In addition, to support my claim, I analyze another aspect of the book, symbolism in Sheean's account of the assassination.

A Journey Like No Other

Sheean's visit to India during 1947-48 turned out like a story. The reason behind the visit, as I have pointed out, was Sheean's hunch that Gandhi's life was about to end. The story is important because it is told by a thoughtful and experienced foreign correspondent, who had met with many world leaders during his career. By 1948, Sheean had already published the best of his books involving foreign reporting. The story is also important because it shows Gandhi in the last few days of his life.

Narrative scholar Marie-Laure Ryan defines a story as follows:

> 1 The mental representation of story involves the construction of the mental image of a world populated with individuated agents (characters) and objects. (Spatial dimension.) 2 This world must undergo not fully predictable changes of state that are caused by non-habitual physical events: either accidents ('happenings') or deliberate actions by intelligent agents. (Temporal dimension.) 3. In addition to being linked to physical states by causal relations, the physical events must be associated with mental states and events (goals, plans, emotions). (347)

The story narrated by Sheean of his visit to India during 1947-48 satisfies the three elements of the definition given above. The story is mainly contained in two chapters. Most of it is in the chapter titled "Upanishad, 1948" (Sheean, *Lead, Kindly* 163); the story continues in the next chapter in which Sheean narrates events after Gandhi's death. The Sanskrit word "Upanishad" "etymologically...suggests 'sitting down near': that is, at the feet of an illumined teacher in an intimate session of spiritual instruction" (Easwaran 19). The chapter title appears to be a deliberate choice (it usually is, but here the case is a little different, so there is a need to state this point). During his interviews, Sheean literally sat next to Gandhi on the floor, after pacing the room with him (Sheean, *Lead, Kindly* 183-184). And Sheean did receive what he thought was spiritual instruction (193). Additionally, during their first interview, Gandhi mentioned a Hindu scripture called *Isha Upanishad*. In fact, he summoned a copy, but it was not an English translation. Sheean found one after Gandhi's death (190, 216). Finally, the year was 1948.

The story begins with Sheean describing his past familiarity with Gandhi and India. The 1930 Salt March had a positive effect on Sheean (Sheean, *Lead, Kindly* 164). He went to India in 1944 as part of his job in the United States Army Air Force, which he had joined in 1942 (Sheean, *Lead, Kindly* 165; Sheean, *Between the Thunder* 421). But Sheean writes that he "was obscurely afraid" of India (Sheean, *Lead, Kindly* 165). He was also afraid of Gandhi, whose ideas seemed mysterious to him (4). Sheean mentions his disappointment with the newly created United Nations, which seemed to be used to amplify—rather than resolve—conflicts (5). On the occasion of India's independence in August 1947, Sheean sent a written "message" to the India League of America (166). The message highlighted India's spiritual strength and the long continuity of its culture. It ended by asking all Indians, regardless of their religious beliefs, to pray for the new country.

The riots following India's partition and the resultant loss of life focused Sheean's attention on the subcontinent, now two independent countries (167). Specifically, Sheean grew increasingly anxious about Gandhi, who had been striving to unite Hindus and Muslims. Sheean writes that "my own interest was centered about Gandhi, because by this time I was well aware of his great spirit and what it had done in the world" (168). However, Sheean was afraid that it might have been "too late" to meet Gandhi: "martyrdom was upon him" (168). Around this time, in late fall of 1947, Sheean talked to the editor of the *Holiday* magazine about his hunch concerning Gandhi and his desire to visit India (168-169). The editor was persuaded and agreed to sponsor Sheean's visit (169).

Sheean left for India in November 1947 (169). He had many stopovers, however, and first reached Pakistan. There he remained until early January, when news about Gandhi's imminent fast reminded him of his purpose for the visit, and Sheean hurried to Delhi (170). After reaching Delhi, Sheean called on the prime minister, Jawaharlal Nehru, to arrange for a meeting with Gandhi (172-173). He also attended Gandhi's evening prayer meetings, standing behind the assembled throng and once with an Indian friend who translated

Gandhi's remarks (178, 181). On January 20, an attempt was made on Gandhi's life. This incident confirmed Sheean's forebodings. He recorded in his diary: "Some great climax in the sacred drama which he is (partly consciously, partly unconsciously) enacting...is surely approaching" (176).

On January 27, Sheean met with Gandhi for the first time. He asked Gandhi questions about *The Bhagavad Gita*, specifically Gandhi's own interpretation of the book, which he had been reading (183). "How can a righteous battle produce a catastrophic result?" Sheean asked Gandhi, referring to the Second World War (183). "If violent means are used there will be a bad result," Gandhi replied (184). Gandhi insisted that non-violence was supreme, admitting, however, that his interpretation of *The Bhagavad Gita* as an allegory upholding non-violence was not the general view. Sheean then proceeded to discuss a number of different topics with Gandhi, among them democracy, "disciplinary resolutions," Indian philosophy, and Gandhi's "inner voice" (186-189). When the meeting ended, Sheean felt deeply moved (193). Gandhi had plainly explained to him a few concepts from Indian philosophy about which he wanted to know, something unique in his experience involving conversations about philosophy (192-193). The conversation mollified his spirit, which had suffered during the war years and after observing what he saw as an inadequate solution in the United Nations (193-195, 4-5).

Sheean met with Gandhi again on January 28 (196). Gandhi told him about Harishchandra, a truthful king, mentioned in *The Mahabharata* (197). Gandhi also remembered his wife, who had died a few years ago, and her role in convincing him to drink goat milk for health reasons after "the cruel manner of milking cows and buffaloes had impelled Gandhi to abjure milk forever" (196-197; Fischer, *The Life of Mahatma* 159). On January 29, Sheean was to accompany Nehru on a trip to Amritsar, Punjab (Sheean, *Lead, Kindly* 199). He told Gandhi that he would not be able to come the next day because of the visit. Gandhi smiled and "raised...his hands," as if "blessing" Sheean, and said, "Go! Go!" (199).

Sheean mentions several conversational qualities of Gandhi, including gestures, expressions, mannerisms, and voice. For example, at different points in their conversation, Sheean noticed Gandhi's "grimace" (198), a "glowing smile" (199), an "anxious and pitying and earnest manner" (192), a "curiously agile movement" (190), his "gentle...voice" (186), and a "birdlike," tilted head (183). These are the types of details that are used in literary journalism (Wolfe 32).

On January 30, Sheean returned to Birla House, in time for Gandhi's prayer meeting (Sheean, *Lead, Kindly* 200-202). He planned to continue their conversations after the meeting. As Sheean waited for Gandhi, who was uncharacteristically late, he talked to the BBC reporter Bob Stimson (202). Finally, Sheean saw Gandhi walk toward the prayer ground across the lawn. The Mahatma had come up to a few steps that led to the slightly elevated prayer ground. Then,

Sheean heard the shots (203). Frightened, he said, "Not the Mahatma" (203). Sheean "recoiled upon the brick wall and leaned against it" and "felt the consciousness of the Mahatma leave" him (203). His eyes were filled with "tears," and there appeared "blisters" on his fingers (203-204). He registered half-consciously a doctor's arrival on the scene, people taking the mortally wounded Gandhi inside the house, and the emptying of the garden (204-205). He walked in the dark and empty garden, once noticing a label next to some flowers (206). He sat on the steps of a building behind the room in which Gandhi now lay (206). Sheean lingered "in the garden" for a long time until Edgar Snow arrived, and then they left Birla House (207).

Scholars of history Louis L. Snyder and Richard B. Morris call Sheean's narration of Gandhi's assassination "a more impressionistic account" compared to the news report about the event that they included in their anthology titled *A Treasury of Great Reporting: 'Literature under Pressure' from the Sixteenth Century to Our Own Time* (723). The news report in the anthology was by "James Michaels, United Press staff writer."

Sheean traveled in the special train carrying the urn containing Gandhi's ashes for their immersion in the confluence of the holy rivers in Allahabad (Sheean, *Lead, Kindly* 219-220). Earlier, he visited the plain where Gandhi was cremated on January 31 (213-214). On the train journey, Sheean noted his observations in a diary: "In empty fields, at small villages and at crossroads it was even more impressive to see the peasants standing with their hands joined in the attitude of prayer...as the train passed" (220). Describing his reaction to Mahatma Gandhi's assassination, Edgar Snow, who was not with Sheean on this train journey, writes, "It was the only time I ever saw a whole nation lose a father and mourn with the contrition of a son who had done the killing" (398). Sheean had difficulty getting out of the massive throngs that surrounded him after he had "seen Gandhiji to the river" (Sheean, *Lead, Kindly* 222). Finally, he found two American teachers from a local Christian college (223). Together, they hired a boat and sailed across the river to reach Allahabad (223-224). Sheean went to Almora, a Himalayan retreat, to reflect on the life-changing experience (234). By his own admission, he was a changed man: "I had two facts which nothing on earth could shake: blisters on my fingers and a realization of God" (230). Explaining the term "God," Sheean writes that it refers to "another [perhaps higher] field: no more" (230).

Returning to Marie-Laure Ryan's definition of a story, after this summary of the story of Sheean's 1947-48 journey to India, it is clear that the story satisfies the three elements specified in the definition. The story contains a world with different characters (Sheean, his *Holiday* magazine editor, Nehru, Gandhi, Sheean's Indian friends, Edgar Snow, and American teachers, among others) and a "spatial dimension" (various places such as Pakistan, Delhi, Amritsar,

Allahabad, among others, not to mention different locations within these places) (Ryan 347). This world of the story (the actual world, too) underwent "changes" that were "not fully predictable" and "caused by non-habitual physical events" (Gandhi's assassination) (347). Finally, "the physical events" gave rise to "mental states" (Sheean's bodily and mental response to the assassination, his realizations after reflecting on what had happened, and the reaction of the masses to the train carrying the ashes) (347).

The story of Sheean's journey to India in 1947-48 is effective for several reasons. One reason is that the story is narrated chronologically. Writer Theodore A. Rees Cheney describes the value of this structure in the following words: "A chronologic structure...brings contentment to the mind. It brings closure, which psychologists say the human mind naturally seeks....Our comfort comes [also]...from the linear development" (143). Two, Sheean gives us Gandhi's speech, although he reminds the reader that he is not quoting the Mahatma verbatim (Sheean, *Lead, Kindly* 192). Three, Sheean gives details that make Gandhi real for the reader: Gandhi's mannerisms (his head-tilting, the raising of his hands in a manner of giving blessings, his leaning "forward" while sitting to stress a point) (186), his practice of walking inside the room as a form of exercise (182), his smile and laughter, his phrases ("On the contrary") (182), his Hindi expressions ("*Acha, acha*") (183).

Finally, although much has been written about the manner of Gandhi's assassination, Sheean's account has a simplicity and clarity that seems closer to the truth. One moment Gandhiji was walking "over the grass" (Sheean, *Lead, Kindly* 204), and the next moment the assassin's bullets ended his life. Rather than describing, as many accounts of the assassination do, how the assassin committed his dark deed, Sheean describes the sound of the bullets: "four small, dull, dark explosions" (203). The pithy description connects the reader to the moment of the assassination.

Sheean writes about his condition after the assassination in a deeply personal way. This narration requires a few readings. His narration of the journey to see the immersion of Gandhi's ashes is vivid. Sheean reflects on his changed worldview because of Gandhi, stating that he saw events such as Hitler's rise as accidental, as a historical phenomenon similar to and different from other such phenomena (232). But the assassination of Gandhi, coupled with his statements about his strong belief in God (however one knows this power), compelled Sheean to reconsider his views rooted in materialism.

As to Gandhi's contribution, Sheean distinguishes between Gandhi's role in India—which was enormous—and his meaning for the world (*Lead, Kindly* 241). He considers satyagraha—truth force—as Gandhi's greatest accomplishment (244). Sheean thinks it extraordinary that this method to resolve conflicts was tested by Gandhi during the same time the world discovered its most potent weapon of destruction (246). About whether *satyagraha* can be applied on a mass scale in the west, Sheean thinks it is difficult because of the cultural, social, and economic factors (245). However, he believes that individual applications of *satyagraha* are not unsuitable for the west and can benefit both the west and the world (246, 252).

Although Sheean states that he came to believe in God after Gandhi's assassination, he avoids giving details about his own religious belief. Like Gandhi, whom Sheean considers his teacher, Sheean is content to point out that people can worship based on their faith (256). Sheean mentions the important roles both the Sermon on the Mount and *The Bhagavad-Gita* played in Gandhi's life. But he credits Gandhi's Hindu background as his primary influence (295). In his biography of Gandhi, Louis Fischer also states that Gandhi combined his reading of *The Gita* with the Sermon on the Mount (*The Life of Mahatma* 96).

Symbolism in Sheean's Story

Literary journalism scholars consider symbolism as a characteristic of such a journalism (Sims "The Literary Journalists"; Lounsberry *Writing Creative*). Sims explains symbolism as "the inner meaning…for a writer" and "deep structures" (22). Lounsberry equates symbolism with "suggestive images" and "subtle resonances" (122). Roland Bartel, an English scholar, defines symbols in the following way: "A symbol does not ask a reader to merge two concepts but rather to let one thing suggest another. A symbol derives its meaning through development and consensus.…A symbol is strengthened by repetition" (61). Symbols "deepen the meaning" (66). Bartel suggests a few "ways of identifying symbols": "repetition," "connotation," and "allusion" (62-68).

A good candidate for a symbol in Sheean's story of his 1947-48 visit to India is Sheean's belief, expressed a number of times, that Gandhi's death was preordained, as part of a historical pattern with outstanding individuals (Sheean, *Lead, Kindly* 233), the kind who come to belong to "all times and all places," as historian Judith M. Brown writes about Gandhi (394). Another symbolic possibility is the notion of God (or god). In Sheean's story, much of it narrated in two chapters, this notion is mentioned several times. However, a strong symbol—and one that perhaps more closely matches Bartel's sense of the concept—is a statement by Gandhi that Sheean remembers repeatedly after the assassination and to which he devises a mental response. The statement, something Gandhi said during his first meeting with Sheean, is as follows: "Kurukshetra is in the heart of man" (Sheean, *Lead, Kindly* 235). To this assertion, Sheean formed a mental response after Gandhi's death: "And there let it remain." The two statements occurred repeatedly to Sheean following the assassination of Gandhi.

Taken together, the two statements—Gandhi's and Sheean's mental response—meet the requirement of repetition in Bartel's criteria for symbols. Additionally, the statements have wider connotations, and, as Bartel states, "fairly definite extra meanings" (63). Finally, Gandhi's statement is an allusion to the battlefield in the Hindu epic *The Mahabharata*. The epic tells the story of a war between brothers from two warrior families, Pandavas and Kauravas. Kurukshetra (literally, a region or area of the Kurus—the people of the Kuru clan) is the battleground on which the war is fought. In India, the name of Kurukshetra is often used suggestively to imply any battle involving fundamental values or principles.

Kurukshetra—the battlefield in *The Mahabharata*—in Gandhi's statement synecdochically alludes to the battle between good and evil in every human heart. Gandhi preferred a figurative interpretation of the battle because of his unyielding belief in non-violence. It may be called an interpretation by "life rather than [by]...literature" (Sheean, *Lead, Kindly* 298). Sheean refers to Gandhi's interpretation of *The Bhagavad Gita* (or *The Gita*), which is part of *The Mahabharata*. *The Gita* is the divine discourse by Krishna delivered on the battlefield of Kurukshetra. Sheean's response to Gandhi's statement about Kurukshetra, "there let it remain" (235), seems to stem from his strong desire for peace in the world, which is clear from Sheean's journey to India, his questions to Gandhi, and his earlier memoirs in which he condemns fascism and tyranny.

In *Lead, Kindly Light*, Sheean notes the catastrophically destructive power of atomic weapons (247), a topic he puts before Gandhi as a question (188). Sheean surely preferred a battle in a person's heart—that is, between an individual's virtues and vices—versus a war in the world. Sheean's journey to India was by itself evidence that he wanted to find ways to prevent wars: "withered were the garlands of the war" (4). Edgar Snow notes Gandhi's role in "growth toward world unity without war" (404). Reviewing the book, Unni Nayar writes that "Sheean saw in Mahatma Gandhi's nonviolent struggle 'a moral alternative to war'" (476). Thus the repeated pairing of Gandhi's statement and Sheean's mental response appears to symbolize peace.

Conclusion

Lead, Kindly Light was chosen by the Book-of-the-Month Club in 1949 (Johnson 605; Immerwahr). In his review of the book for *The New York Times*, Louis Fischer writes: "The seventy-four pages describing Sheean's progress to faith are subjective, honest and revealing; here is a monograph, in effect, on Western man in pain. These pages constitute a poignant sequel to Sheean's 'Personal History,' and this section is the heart of the book. It is Sheean at his best, writing about himself in the perspective of universal problems" ("Light from India" 3, 24). The pages Fischer refers to include most of the story of Sheean's 1947-48 trip to India that I have analyzed in this chapter. In another review of the book, Nayar praises Sheean's perception and writing: "His sensitive, profound mind grasped Gandhi's truth in much less time than others have taken to perceive it, and he has interpreted it in language at once brilliant and appealing" (475).

According to Sims, "literary journalism stands as a humanistic approach to culture as compared to the scientific, abstract, or indirect approach taken by much standard journalism" (*True Stories* 12). In his 1984 book, Sims refers to varied cultures: "The literary quality of these works comes from the collision of worlds, from a confrontation with the symbols of another, real culture" ("The Literary Journalists" 4). Similarly, the website of the Lettre Ulysses Award for the Art of Reportage calls on literary journalists to understand "historical background"; "comprehend heterogeneity"; "reconcile different layers of information"; and explore different "cultures," "traditions," and "mentalities" ("The Art of Reportage"). When evaluated against these aims and values of literary journalism, *Lead, Kindly Light* fares well. It introduces readers (mainly western readers) to a different culture. But perhaps equally important, the book shows the reader a side of Gandhi not often found in books about him: Gandhi in a conversation. What Sheean has done is perhaps unequaled. He had a most unusual premonition, followed it to India, and was present—inexplicably—when Gandhi was assassinated. Even if one does not find the book as a whole to be an example of literary journalism, Sheean's story and its symbolism analyzed here should be seen as a work of literary journalism.

Chapter 6
In Defense of a Practical Idealist

In *Nehru: The Years of Power*, Vincent Sheean defends a pragmatic leader, Jawaharlal Nehru, and his newly independent nation, India. Sheean can call both entities, the leader and the nation he leads, his friends. Sheean published a personal tribute to Gandhi in *Lead, Kindly Light* and interviewed Mahatma Gandhi hours before his assassination on January 30, 1948. In this book on Nehru, Sheean writes about his conversations and interactions with India's political leaders, including and especially with Jawaharlal Nehru. He has not just met India's political leaders, he has seen India in a substantive way, to understand it a little better as a foreign correspondent. For example, giving credit to Nehru for working hard to improve the country, Sheean writes the following: "I have traveled far more in India than most people ever do, Indian or foreign, and I have yet to see any work, plant, enterprise, school, hospital or laboratory which he [Nehru] has not visited" (*Nehru: The Years* 70). Literary journalist Ted Conover, among other scholars of the form, emphasizes immersion as a principal characteristic of this type of journalism. In this book, Sheean shows the reader that he is involved in his subject of journalistic inquiry and writing. For instance, he lists industrial establishments, infrastructural projects, and scientific and social agencies connected to the "Five Year Plan" that he visited (*Nehru: The Years* 60-61).

The book is organized thematically. The first chapter looks back at India's recent past, specifically the person of Mahatma Gandhi, who more than anyone else defined the country. The reader reads about an annual gathering of some of Gandhi's friends and associates, including chiefly Nehru, at Birla House on the morning of January 30. The chapter then makes some preliminary remarks about Nehru. In chapter two, Sheean uses a symbol of a "potter" and a "welder" (80) to discuss India's five-year plans. Chapter three describes the situation in Kashmir. Sheean has met with two principal Kashmiri leaders, Sheikh Mohammad Abdullah and Bakshi Ghulam Muhammad (108). In the chapter, Sheean briefly discusses the reasons for the Kashmir problem. In the fourth chapter, Sheean analyzes India's (Nehru's) foreign policy. The book offers a clear explanation of India's decisions on international issues and crises. In the next four chapters, Sheean briefly examines Nehru's political strengths, reorganization of Indian states based on regional languages, some of Nehru's associates, and Jawaharlal Nehru as an individual. At the end of the book, there is a small working paper

Nehru himself drafted, a philosophical exposition about governance and leadership focused on India.

The book has a few brief narratives: a scene, an anecdote, a conversation. But it is predominantly discursive, expository. It is important to remember, however, that Hartsock mentions "discursive literary journalism" (*A History* 114). *Nehru: The Years of Power* reads like a long essay, lightly sketched. However, there are some parts that can be read as literary journalism. One is the symbol of a potter and a welder to connect India of the past with India of the present. The second part is the chapter discussing India's foreign policy. This chapter is discursive, but it has an impressive clarity, based partly on Sheean's conversations with Nehru, and a comparison of India's situation to the early years of the United States. Finally, the last part that reads like literary journalism and that I will also analyze is Sheean's portrayal of Jawaharlal Nehru as an individual.

To show how consciously Sheean practiced immersion, consider this quote from his chapter on Kashmir: "Within a single day in Srinagar, the dreamy capital of the little state, I came to understand more of the peculiarity of the Kashmir situation than would have been possible…by the study of a decade's debate" (*Nehru: The Years* 86-87). As we have seen, empathy for subjects of journalistic inquiry and writing is another characteristic of literary journalism (Hartsock, *Literary Journalism* 19-20). Richard Filloy, a scholar of English, praises George Orwell for his empathy in his journalism and political writing:

> The careful manipulation of character may be seen as an important ingredient in the rhetoric of political writing. For such writing to survive the occasion which begets it, it needs an appeal which is not topical. The writer's character is just such an appeal: a good man is still admirable and interesting even when his specific context is gone. Such characters attract audiences by exemplifying values that transcend time and place: honesty, loyalty, empathy, and humility in Orwell's case. (66-67)

Sheean's empathy can especially be seen in the chapter on India's foreign policy, as I will discuss.

The Symbol of a "Potter" and a "Welder"

In chapter two, Sheean tries to connect the old, pre-independence—or even historical—India with the India that is newly emerging or taking shape. He describes an incident during a car trip including him and "a government official" from Mahabalipuram to Madras (now Chennai) (Sheean, *Nehru: The Years* 46). The driver sees a potter giving finishing touches to a large clay pot and suggests to Sheean that he may want to take a look. After seeing the potter and his pot, Sheean is unable to forget this village worker. Sheean notes the potter's skill, his absorption in his work, his quiet manner. Sheean thinks about

In Defense of a Practical Idealist 99

the fact that he is born into this occupation and that generations of his ancestors practiced the same trade, going back centuries. After this part-journalistic, part-anthropological experience, Sheean continues to Madras in the car. Sheean mentions the incident to a prominent Congress leader, C. Rajagopalachari (known as Rajaji), a former freedom fighter and the first governor-general of independent India (47). The ageing leader, whom Sheean respects, does not seem to think much of the potter.

Then, Sheean visits a railroad "coach factory" and comes across a young welder from a nearby village but "trained in Switzerland." Sheean asks the engineer who is giving him a tour whether the welder's father is a potter (48). The engineer laughs and replies that he may have to inquire about it. Later, Sheean briefly meets with the director of the enterprise. The potter he saw in the village is still on his mind. He tells the director that a village potter may feel out of place in the factory (49). The director philosophically responds that India is full of contradictions. Then, an engineer in the room says the following about a potter, contrasting his job with that of a factory worker: "He can sing a song. Perhaps he is a little freer." Other officials present also join the conversation. On his visit to Rajaji again, Sheean once more brings up the potter (50). Rajaji becomes excited and criticizes the Indian government's approach to industrialization. He points out that because of the current industrialization drive the potter's son may move to a town, thereby depriving his family and village of an occupational worker, which may lead to an increase in price for pots in the village (50-51).

Next in the chapter, Sheean describes various industrial establishments, irrigation projects, and other agencies he visited across India (60-64). He tells the reader that he disagrees with Rajaji and agrees with Nehru that India's future lies with industrialization (51). Industrialization, Sheen says, is important because agriculture in India depends on monsoon, which can be uncertain.

Sheean ends the chapter by invoking Mahatma Gandhi: "None of this [planned industrialization pursued by the Indian government] is specifically in Gandhiji's language but it is...further development of his language" (80). Sheean recalls Gandhi's famous statement about Nehru: "He will speak my language after I am gone." Sheean then compares Gandhi to the potter and Nehru to the welder, writing that "the welder is the son of the potter."

According to Bartel, "a symbol expands language" (61). It has a power of suggestion. The potter in this chapter symbolizes India's rural past and present. This rural life has (or had) advantages, a simple life, for example. But it also has large numbers of people living a life of economic hardship. The welder suggests India's present and future, an actor and participant in the hard work of industrial development, with its promises and potential for economic successes. Sheean acknowledges that the present focus on industrial progress in India is different from the vision of India that Mahatma Gandhi had. Fischer describes the type of economic development Gandhi envisioned:

> If India were to carry out most of Gandhi's numerous economic prescriptions the result, two or three decades after his death, might be an economy pivoting on a fully employed, self-governing village enjoying maximum self-sufficiency and minimum mechanization; a city where capitalists and...governments shared industry and trade; strong trade unions and co-operatives. (*The Life of Mahatma* 332)

It is clear that Gandhi's preferred way of economic progress aimed at balancing industrialization with self-sufficiency of villages. Sheean believes that Nehru's focus on industrialization is an extension of Gandhi's wish to improve poor Indians' living conditions. The symbols of a potter and a welder work to the extent that they represent a rural and an urban setting, respectively. The two symbols are evocative, but they do not communicate nuances and complexities of the two dissimilar economic visions.

Newly-Independent India's Foreign Policy

In chapter four, Sheean makes a cogent case for India's foreign policy, an area with which he is more at home. He explains the rationale for the policy succinctly: "India's pursuit of peace is not only ideological or philosophical: it wears the aspect of necessity" (*Nehru: The Years* 157). Sheean points out that India has two large neighbors to its north, China and Russia, who have powerful militaries (156-157). India also has a hostile neighbor to its northwest, Pakistan. Sheean lists three main objectives of India's foreign policy, as conceived by Nehru: "nonalignment," "the pursuit of peace when possible," and "national interest" (127). Finally, Sheean states that India wants to pursue socialism, unlike western democracies, but would like to do so remaining democratic, unlike Russia and China (149).

Defending India's desire to remain friendly with all countries, sometimes even by avoiding condemning a transgression, Sheean draws the reader's attention to the U. S. foreign policy in its early years. Sheean quotes from a speech by George Washington: "Observe faith and justice toward all nations. Cultivate peace and harmony with all....In the execution of such a plan nothing is more essential than that permanent inveterate antipathies against particular nations and passionate attachments for others should be excluded" (125). Sheean then tells the reader that "it does seem strange that Americans grow impatient with others for doing and believing what we did and believed for most of our existence as a nation" (124).

Sheean clarifies that India's foreign policy is realistic. It seeks high aims when it can but settles for what it can get at other times: "We do not like it...but we must put up with it," as Nehru says (160). Perhaps because Sheean was a foreign correspondent and knew something about foreign affairs, Sheean's argument for India's foreign policy in this chapter reads clearly and persuasively. His quoting from George Washington's speech, Nehru's books and speeches, his conversations with Nehru, and his analysis of current events in India make this chapter engaging and informative.

Nehru as an Individual

In the last chapter of the book, Sheean offers an interesting analysis of Jawaharlal Nehru. Referring to a point made by Frank Moraes in his book *Jawaharlal Nehru* that "the Prime Minister is a lonely man," Sheean says that the loneliness belongs to Nehru's "position," not to him personally (*Nehru: The Years* 267). In an earlier chapter, Sheean describes an incident in 1958 when he went to the prime minister's residence to meet with Nehru (192-193). Mr. Nehru had gone to a "parliamentary party meeting" to try to convince his colleagues to let him leave his post for a short time, as a "trial" (192). When Nehru returned, Sheean "knew from his manner and his words that he had again…yielded to the wishes of the majority" (193).

Sheean tells the reader that Nehru is not an "orator" (277). Referring to his famous speech in the constituent assembly on India's independence and another when Gandhi was assassinated, Sheean states that these speeches were made "under…overwhelming emotion" (277). He informs that Nehru's "talks in public are as natural and unpretentious as his talk in private" (278). Phillips Talbot, an American scholar working for a New York-based organization for international affairs, has this to say about Nehru's speaking style when he met Nehru in 1939: "For a mass orator his voice is surprisingly soft, modulated, personal" (54; Nanda 10-11).

Sheean mentions that he accompanied Nehru to Calcutta to receive ancient Buddhist "relics" (*Nehru: The Years* 196). Sheean describes the prime minister's house and offices in various buildings (262-264). He briefly tells the reader that he chatted with the prime minister's daughter, Indira, later a prime minister herself, while waiting for him (193). These privileges show a certain amount of trust between Jawaharlal Nehru and Vincent Sheean. Johnson notes that Nehru respected Sheean's views (666). It is this closeness between an American journalist and the prime minister of India that makes Sheean's observations insightful. Not only did Sheean talk to Mr. Nehru, he saw him at his speeches, traveled with him, went to his house, and read his books, among other things. To anyone interested in Jawaharlal Nehru, Sheean's portrait is revealing. For example, Sheean describes Nehru's face as "expressive, always changing" (268). Such a detail can only come after a good deal of observation.

Conclusion

Reviewing the book in *The New York Times*, Louis Fischer praises Sheean for "a revealing close-up of the great leader" toward the book's end ("Highlights and Shadows" 28). However, Fischer also criticizes Sheean for glossing over India's repeated "abstain" votes at the United Nations (6). *Nehru: The Years of Power* is an interesting account of the first decade of India's independence. Despite the book's coverage of wide-ranging issues, the reader finds the portraits of important political leaders besides Nehru cursory. With the exception of a few chapters (the one on foreign policy and the one on Nehru as an individual), the rest of the chapters seem lightly sketched. Even though the book focused on the prime minister, a few leading members of his cabinet could have been dealt with in more depth. Some of these leaders, who are mentioned in the book, include Pundit Govind Ballabh Pant (the home minister), Morarji Desai (the finance minister), and V. K. Krishna Menon (the defense minister). As a consequence, although the book repeatedly stresses Nehru's democratic inclinations and values—and credibly so—the book is ironically closer to drawing a portrait of someone like a philosopher king. As I have argued above, some parts of the book (the potter and welder symbols, foreign policy, Nehru as an individual), along with Sheean's immersion in its research and writing and his empathy toward his research or subjects, make for good arguments for the book to be seen, at least in part, as a work of literary journalism.

Chapter 7
Conclusion

In an interview published in *The New York Times* dated December 6, 1974, Vincent Sheean told the interviewer, reporter Israel Shenker, a truism about himself: "I'm talking about the world—it's the only thing I know about" (Shenker, "Vincent Sheean at 75" 41). A little more than three months later, Vincent Sheean died (Montgomery). In a career spanning about 35 years (the most active, journalistic career), Sheean wrote detailed, comprehensive, personal volumes—not just stories but connected historical and contextual analyses—about events in France, Spain, Britain, Czechoslovakia, Italy, Austria, northern Morocco, China, Russia, and India. His preferred format was books, though he also wrote numerous articles and news reports (see Johnson, pages 740-754, for an extensive list of Vincent Sheean's publications; a short, books-only bibliography is presented in Appendix 1 of this book).

His five journalistic, nonfiction books that I have analyzed contain a lot of information (some more than others). They include, in varying degrees, stories and episodes, characters and scenes, and descriptions and details. Sheean told doctoral student Carl Edward Johnson, who interviewed him for his thesis, that good writers have "a respect for language" (Johnson 718-719). Among the books I analyzed, Sheean's highly developed linguistic craftsmanship is most evident in *Personal History* and *Not Peace but a Sword*. But it is also present in *Between the Thunder and the Sun; Lead, Kindly Light;* and *Nehru: The Years of Power*.

Through my analysis of his five journalistic, nonfiction books, I have shown that Vincent Sheean was a literary journalist. The evidence for this claim is the books' stories and scenes, well-crafted structures and sentences, imagery and symbolism, and lifelike characters and vivid descriptions. The evidence also comes from immersion by Sheean in his journalistic settings, his empathy for his research subjects or characters (or people he met or described), and his interactions with individuals and leaders from different cultures.

Personal History and *Not Peace but a Sword* should be seen as works of literary journalism because of their stories and scenes and skilled, artistic writing. The other three books I have analyzed—*Between the Thunder and the Sun; Lead, Kindly Light*; and *Nehru: The Years of Power*—have parts showing qualities of literary journalism: scenes, characters, story, imagery, symbolism, clarity.

Distinguishing memoirs and "immersion writing," Ted Conover states, a "classic memoir is about what happened to me more than what I actively investigated so that I could write about it" (15). In immersion writing, the "focus is always outwards." The five journalistic, nonfiction books (at least four of them memoirs of some sort) by Sheean that I examined have their focus outwards. It is true, as Gornick points out, that effective writers of true stories frame and compose them mainly through their subjectivity. However, Sheean demonstrates that subjectivity and outward focus can fuse (which is what Gornick recommends as well). In the following quote, John Maxwell Hamilton describes the essentials of Sheean's work: "Although Sheean was uncomfortable within the traditional norms of journalism, he still was essentially a reporter. He searched for facts...Sheean brought expert observation skills to his reporting. He told the reader what he saw, the conditions under which he saw it, and what it meant" (*Journalism's Roving* 215).

In his journalistic, nonfiction books, Sheean combined literary techniques with skillful journalism relying on observation, interactions, conversations, interviews, meetings, travel, reading, diary writing (though he was not a regular diary writer), and general knowledge of societies and cultures—their tastes and preferences, customs and traditions, past and present. He did not shirk from risky reporting opportunities, as is perhaps most prominently seen in his reporting about the Rif. He also went to see a Chinese warlord at a time when it was risky for foreign reporters to travel in China. But he did not take risks that were unnecessary or merely to obtain fame. He was too cerebral for that.

Each of the five books I analyzed contains a world by itself, during a period. *Personal History* tells us about the world in the 1920s: the Rif war, the failed communist revolution in China, and the 1929 riots in former Palestine. Christopher Daly calls this decade "the heyday of the big-city daily newspaper" (188). *Not Peace but a Sword* and *Between the Thunder and the Sun* narrate and describe the precarious 1930s (*Between the Thunder* . . . also covers the early years of the 1940s): the Spanish civil war, Nazi Germany, the attack on Pearl Harbor. Christopher Daly, again, puts his finger on the main point: "In the 1930s and early 1940s, the news started off bad and just kept getting worse" (217). Finally, in *Lead, Kindly Light* and *Nehru: The Years of Power*, Sheean wrote about an ancient civilization and a new nation. In the first of the two books, he wrote about "a man of vision and action, who asked many of the profoundest questions that face humankind" (Brown 394). The experience behind the book was unlike anything Sheean had witnessed. The second book wove disparate constituents of culture, politics, and settings significantly different from Sheean's own.

Sims calls literary journalism a "humanistic" endeavor (*True Stories* 12). This description fits Sheean's journalism. In *Personal History*, he announces his desire to find connections between his own life and lives of others with whom he shares the world (Sheean, *Personal History* 397). Sheean also states that he likes finding out about the core struggles facing different people, nations (187-188). The first journalistic, nonfiction book Sheean wrote was about the Rif, and two of his last such books were connected with India. Among leaders or distinguished individuals he admired were Abd el-Krim, Borodin, Gandhi, and Mme Sun Yat-sen, each from a different part of the world. Sheean defended democracy and condemned fascism. At the end of *Not Peace but a Sword*, he writes that he could not sleep thinking about the impending defeat of the Spanish republic (Sheean, *Not Peace* 345-346). He traveled on the train that carried Gandhi's ashes. His agony at Gandhi's assassination was not unlike—if not more than—his pain at the passing of Rayna Prohme, whom he cherished, twenty-one years earlier.

There is another sense in which the term "humanistic" is applicable to Sheean. Writer Walker Percy states that humans engage in "symbolic transactions": "talking or listening, gossiping, reading books, writing books, making reports, listening to lecturers, delivering lectures, telling jokes, looking at paintings" (119). Sheean did all of these things and many others.

Given the amount of journalistic, nonfiction writing by Sheean (the five books analyzed here and *This House against This House*—not covered in this book), along with the fact that his writing contains many qualities of literary journalism, it is surprising that Sheean is rarely mentioned as an exemplar of the form. It is also important to realize that the books analyzed here were written over twenty-five years, and each of them combined journalism with artistic writing (some more than others).

In a book review of *Second Read: Writers Look Back at Classic Works of Reportage*, Brian Gabrial, a journalism scholar, states that "John Maxwell Hamilton's essay...on Vincent Sheean's Personal History persuasively advocates for its resuscitation in the canon" (143). In my review of literary journalism scholarship, I came across only one book, Applegate's collection of literary journalism writers and editors, which included a brief biographical entry on Vincent Sheean. Weber mentions Sheean in passing (*The Literature* 57), and Michael J. Arlen refers to him in a couple of sentences ("Notes"). Part of the paradox between a meritorious case for Sheean as a literary journalist and his relative obscurity in scholarship of the form may be due to Sheean himself.

Hamilton writes that Sheean's ideas of "reaching an accommodation with the Soviet Union" after the Second World War "did not fit postwar America" (*Journalism's Roving* 216). To quote Sheean himself from his last world-spanning memoir (in continuation of *Personal History*, *Not Peace but a Sword*, and *Between the Thunder and the Sun*), *This House against This House*, published in 1945:

> It is my conviction that no such division of the world is necessary or desirable, that the two systems are susceptible of modification, that synthesis is the inevitable law of development, and that those who try to set forth or encourage a *deliberate* antagonism between capitalism as it

stands in America and socialism as it stands in the Soviet Union are enemies of humanity. (Sheean, *This House against* 68)

Whatever position one may take on Sheean's words above, it is clear from the recent events that the idea of two opposed camps in the world—a democratic world order led by the United States against Russia with its continuing ruminations of the former Soviet Union—is not conducive to a peaceful world. I will elaborate a bit on this point later. But it should be noted here that this topic is both vast and complex, and my only intention here is to point out a need for better foreign journalism in light of a tremendous potential for harm resulting from inflexible polarization and antagonism between strong nations.

Hamilton also mentions changes in reading preferences of Americans after the Second World War as another reason Sheean's popularity declined ("Not one of the ten books on the *Publishers Weekly* best-seller list in 1949, the year Sheean's *Lead, Kindly Light* appeared, was by a journalist, let alone a foreign correspondent") (*Journalism's Roving* 216). In addition, Sheean faced personal problems, and his "name did not automatically open the publishing doors" (216). Cott notes that after the publication of Sheean's memoir *This House against This House* "several ["reviewers"] put Sheean's method of 'personal journalism' on the examination table" (302).

These factors may have played some, perhaps indirect, part in the absence of Sheean in the front row of literary journalism scholarship. However, it is also useful to approach this reality from the other side, that is, from the side of the literary journalism scholarship. Hartsock notes that the form received greater scholarly attention in the 1960s when New Journalism (a type or continuation of literary journalism, as we have seen) appeared (*A History* 191).

If we take a roughly approximate date of the early 1970s—Wolfe's book of New Journalism was published in 1973—as the beginning of the scholarship of this form, these early years were already distant from Sheean's best work by about three decades. That is, by the early 1970s, Sheean's best journalistic, nonfiction books (*Personal History, Not Peace but a Sword*) were about three decades old. Granted that the literary journalism scholarship has noted some authors from the period in which Sheean was most active: the 1930s and 1940s: A. J. Liebling, Ernest Hemingway, Martha Gellhorn (Hartsock, *A History* 170-174). However, it is hardly possible for literary journalism scholars to examine all or even most deserving candidates among those who wrote journalistic nonfiction during this period.

In addition to the existing scholarship of literary journalism, research related to the form continues to expand and grow. It may be sheer lack of acquaintance with Sheean that may be responsible for his relative obscurity in the scholarship of the form. Indeed, in his 1992 anthology, Connery states that he makes "no claim that this book's list of literary journalists is complete"

("Preface" xv). He adds that "to a degree, the writers included here are representative."

I decided to ask a leading historian of the form, Professor John Hartsock, whether he considered Vincent Sheean as a literary journalist when he wrote his history of the genre in 2000. I was fortunate and grateful to receive a reply from him (not just because I did not know him personally but also because he has retired from his academic position). With his permission, I quote most of his reply below:

> When I published *A History [of American Literary Journalism: The Emergence of a Modern Narrative Form]* I did not expect to cover everyone, so congratulations on discovering Vincent Sheean. He sounds fascinating. He wasn't excluded because he wasn't worthy. Applegate's book posed special problems, as I noted in my book. Also, my book was well-along with review by the publisher when I discovered Applegate's book a year or two after it came out. I realized I was not going to be able to do a thorough review of everyone listed, and vet them according to how well I thought they were or were not literary journalists (my views have moderated some over the years). For example, I excluded the other Sheehan, Neil. Applegate provides a very broad view. But at least I wanted to take note of him for future scholars to consult and arrive at their own conclusions.
>
> P.S. Tom Connery is right. Any collection can only be representative. Now you can add Sheean to that collection! (Hartsock "E-mail to the author")

As a corollary to the discussion about Sheean's place (or absence) in the literary journalism canon, I will make a concise case (as I hope to have done indirectly throughout this book) for why he deserves a prominent place in the scholarship of the form.

Vincent Sheean wrote about important world events as human stories involving politicians, officials, people, soldiers, organizations, buildings, cities, town squares and city avenues, rivers and hills, cultural celebrations, individual and mass reactions, conflicts and wars, books and literature, speeches, journalism and writing, cablegrams and articles, history, travel and recuperation, plays and musical performances, dangers and risks, devotion and affection, disgust and alienation, fellow journalists, guides, and leaders. His journalistic prose immerses readers and takes them on a journey across time and place, from place to place, and through a period. This sense of journalism—this education of the world—provides context and understanding, breeds humility and an appreciation of varied perspectives, and promotes compassion and empathy.

Reading a book about a decade, even if through the lens of a single journalist, helps us synthesize our knowledge about the decade, helping us see it better in relation to our time. Reading a strictly fact-based history does not give the same experience. Reading such a history equips us with information, but we have a better grasp of such information if the information is presented to us along with stories, something that Vincent Sheean does in varying degrees in the books analyzed in this book. These stories, along with exposition and analysis, make us see events that happened long ago.

Such foreign journalism is even more needed now in a complex world that is more connected than ever before. Because of great strides in information technology, there is also a high degree of fragmentation in the reception of information by people. Information comes in bits and pieces from numerous sources. So it is difficult for readers (and listeners and viewers, for that matter) to have a vicarious sense of immersion in an event. Tom Fenton, a former foreign correspondent, explains the importance of foreign correspondents in this way: "More than ever, our country is part of 'abroad.' America should be fighting its news industry for the reempowerment of foreign correspondents" (206).

Highlighting several problems with the U.S. news media regarding its coverage of foreign news, Fenton points to missed signals (with regard to Islamic terrorism, for example) (194), "predetermined political and commercial needs" (201), reluctance to cover local or native perspectives due to safety fears (189), "political bias" (192), and "absence of a resident correspondent" (200). Giving an example of the war against terrorism after 9/11, Fenton states, "The lack of a trusted voice...of a veteran foreign correspondent literate in Afghan affairs explaining such things...to American[s]...left average Americans with no serious guide to the war, *nobody to put it all together for them*" (199, my emphasis). Information vacuum resulting from inadequate foreign reporting is exploited by politicians (Fenton 199). In Sheean's books analyzed in this book, Sheean *synthesizes* information about foreign countries and events for American readers (emphasis added). It should be noted that Fenton makes this point in relation to broadcast news, but his concern applies to print journalism as well (though Fenton is less critical of the print news media's coverage and notes a few journalists who did excellent work) (188).

In a quote that brings Vincent Sheean to mind, Fenton emphasizes immersion by foreign reporters in their settings: "Ideally, the point of foreign correspondence is for journalists to make informed judgments after immersing themselves in the actual place" (202).

In what seems a prescient quote today, Fenton mentions a foreign affairs crisis that shows no signs of resolution as I type these words: "Russia's blatant meddling in the rigged and fraudulent 2004 Ukrainian presidential election should have been a warning to us all. Yet much of the American media arrived late on the story and provided little context, failing to identify the development as another example of Russian empire-building" (207).

Vincent Sheean, who reported about the Spanish civil war and predicted the Second World War, immersed himself in the events of Europe and the world in the turbulent 1930s. He connected the dots, went to places with stressors and activities that were bound to fructify in ominous ways, commented on actions by political leaders, observed the situation developing on the ground, paid attention to and thought about reactions of common people and the significance of foreboding events.

He was in India on a hunch that Gandhi's life might end, argued for an empathic understanding of the newly independent India's foreign policy, agreed with the Riffian or the Chinese people about their right to control their own affairs, criticized the Soviet Union for its crackdown on dissenters, and emphasized coming to an understanding with the former Soviet Union to promote a peaceful world. The last point is seen in a quote from Sheean's *This House against This House*—a book not discussed in my analysis here—mentioned earlier.

Finally, a point needs to be made about craft in literary journalism. Sheean's literary journalism, as seen in his voluminous books, is an excellent example of fusion of literary techniques and journalistic skills and work. His books provide a strong rationale for the form and convincingly argue for its value to journalism programs and society. What his books do, above all, is synthesize numerous data points (or information, thought fragments) connected with a foreign event or situation. This synthesis is achieved because of his literary journalism.

Books presenting historical events plainly as scholarly compendia, or stories of mostly subjective impressions in foreign settings, have limited usefulness. The former may inform with facts, leaving out much of what facts alone cannot deliver: impressions, atmosphere, underlying currents, beliefs, errors, and significance. The latter may titillate, entertain, and even inspire, but subjective impressions taken to high limits leave readers with questions about the events themselves, their intricacies, and their significance.

What Sheean offered was a mean between facts or information by itself and predominantly subjective accounts (the kind in which the authorial "I" freely and often deliberately draws attention to itself). With a few exceptions (parts of *Between the Thunder and the Sun* and *Nehru: The Years of Power*, for example), Sheean exercised restraint in regard to his subjective self. He preferred to see events—and people affected by the events—as larger entities guiding his journalism and prose.

Appendix 1:
Select Books by Vincent Sheean

This is an abridged, books-only bibliography of Vincent Sheean. Please note that the books included here are only a selection; Sheean published other books as well. In addition, Sheean published numerous articles, short stories, news reports, and so on. Readers interested in his larger body of work should see an extensive list of his publications given by Carl Edward Johnson in his doctoral thesis titled *A Twentieth Century Seeker: A Biography of James Vincent Sheean* (see pages 740-754).

Memoirs

Personal History (1935)
Not Peace but a Sword (1939)
Between the Thunder and the Sun (1943)
This House against This House (1945)
Lead, Kindly Light (1949)
The Indigo Bunting: A Memoir of Edna St. Vincent Millay (1951) – in part a biography
First and Last Love (1956)
Nehru: The Years of Power (1960) – in part an essay

Biographies

Mahatma Gandhi: A Great Life in Brief (1954)
Orpheus at Eighty (1958) – on Giuseppe Verdi, Italian composer

Novels

Sanfelice (1936)
A Day of Battle (1938)

Appendix 2:
Archival Sources for Vincent Sheean

1. Wisconsin Historical Society, Vincent Sheean Papers, 1933-1980: https://digicoll.library.wisc.edu/cgi/f/findaid/findaid-idx?c=wiarchives;cc=wiarchives;view=text;rgn=main;didno=uw-whs-mss00950
2. Syracuse University, Vincent Sheean Papers: https://library.syracuse.edu/digital/guides/s/sheean_v.htm
3. The University of Chicago Library, the Hanna Holborn Gray Special Collections Research Center. Guide to the Vincent Sheean and Ruth Falkenau Correspondence 1919-1986: https://www.lib.uchicago.edu/e/scrc/findingaids/view.php?eadid=ICU.SPCL.FALKENAUSHEEAN
4. The New York Public Library Archives & Manuscripts. Vincent Sheean Collection of Papers: https://archives.nypl.org/brg/19214
5. The New York Public Library Archives & Manuscripts, Papers about Diana Forbes-Robertson and Vincent Sheean, 1985-88: https://archives.nypl.org/the/21555
6. Yale Collection of American Literature, Beinecke Rare Book and Manuscript Library, Vincent Sheean Letters to Harry E. Maule: https://orbis.library.yale.edu/vwebv/holdingsInfo?bibId=16216719
7. Syracuse University, Dorothy Thompson Papers, Box 27 and 28: https://library.syracuse.edu/digital/guides/t/thompson_d.htm
8. Library of Congress, Edgar Ansel Mowrer and Lilian T. Mowrer Papers, 1898-1978, Correspondence with Vincent Sheean: https://catalog.loc.gov/vwebv/search?searchCode=LCCN&searchArg=mm%2073033803&searchType=1&permalink=y
9. Library of Congress, Eric Sevareid Papers, 1909-1993, Correspondence with Vincent Sheean: https://catalog.loc.gov/vwebv/search?searchCode=LCCN&searchArg=mm%2078039495&searchType=1&permalink=y
10. The Tamiment Library & Robert F. Wagner Labor Archives, James Lardner Papers, Box 1 Folder 12, Vincent Sheean: http://dlib.nyu.edu/findingaids/html/tamwag/alba_067/alba_067.html

Appendix 3:
Two Pages from Sheean's Journal, January 21, 1948

On the next pages there are images of the two pages from Sheean's journal dated January 21, 1948. He records his premonition about the assassination of Mahatma Gandhi on these pages.

Fig. A3.1.a: Two pages from Sheean's journal, January 21, 1948

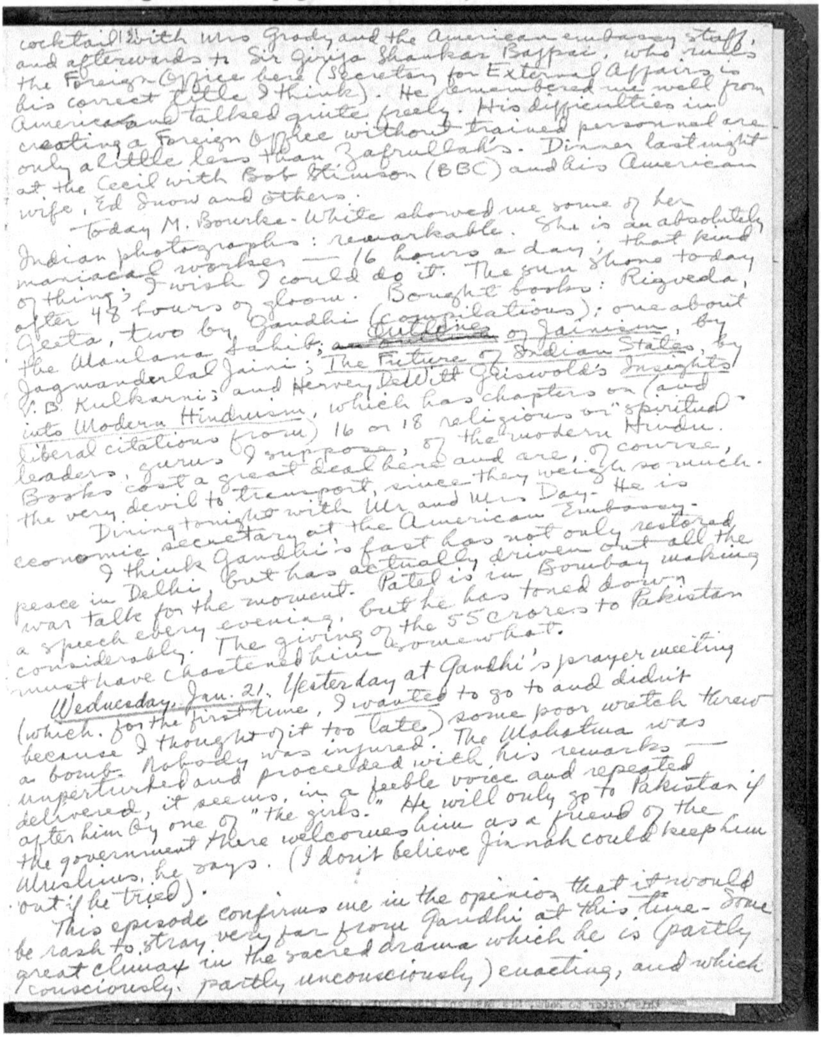

cocktail with Mrs Grady and the American embassy staff, and afterwards to Sir Girija Shankar Bajpai, who rules the Foreign Office here (Secretary for External Affairs is his correct title I think). He remembered us well from America and talked quite freely. His difficulties in creating a Foreign Office without trained personnel are only a little less than Zafrullah's. Dinner last night at the Cecil with Bob Stimson (BBC) and his American wife, Ed Snow and others.

Today M. Bourke-White showed me some of her Indian photographs: remarkable. She is an absolutely maniacal worker — 16 hours a day, that kind of thing; I wish I could do it. The gun I bore today after 48 hours of gloom. Bought books: Rigveda, Geeta, two by Gandhi (compilations); one about the Maulana Sahib, an Outline of Jainism, by Jagmanderlal Jaini; The Future of Indian States, by V. B. Kulkarni; and Hervey DeWitt Griswold's Insights into Modern Hinduism, which has chapters on (and liberal citations from) 16 or 18 religious or "spiritual leaders, gurus, I suppose, of the modern Hindu. Books cost a great deal here and are, of course, the very devil to transport, since they weigh so much.

Dining tonight with Mr and Mrs Day. He is economic secretary at the American Embassy. I think Gandhi's fast has not only restored peace in Delhi, but has actually driven out all the war talk for the moment. Patel is in Bombay making a speech every evening, but he has toned down considerably. The giving of the 55 crores to Pakistan must have chastened him somewhat.

Wednesday, Jan. 21. Yesterday at Gandhi's prayer meeting (which, for the first time, I wanted to go to and didn't because I thought to get it too late) some poor wretch threw a bomb. Nobody was injured. The Mahatma was unperturbed and proceeded with his remarks — delivered, it seems, in a feeble voice and repeated after him by one of "the girls." He will only go to Pakistan if the government there welcomes him as a friend of the Muslims, he says. (I don't believe Jinnah could keep him out if he tried).

This episode confirms me in the opinion that it would be rash to stray very far from Gandhi at this time. Some great climax in the sacred drama which he is (partly consciously, partly unconsciously) enacting, and which

First page. Source: Wisconsin Historical Society, WHI-152588

Appendix 3

Fig. A3.1.b: Two pages from Sheean's journal, January 21, 1948

has been lifted to the tragic height of a last act since August, is surely approaching. The fact that he is so uncannily able, by the instinct of genius, to assist the operation of fate, merely makes this climax inevitable. I have believed since last summer that if he is to be killed it must be (for India's sake) by a Hindu and not by a Muslim. This is in the logic of every sacred drama in the entire history of religion, and I believe it will take place.

Maulana Abul Kalam Azad is ill; Rajendra Prasad was fasting with the Mahatma and needs another two or three days to recover his strength. As these were the leaders I was most anxious to see, I am now again reduced to waiting for a summons. The newspapers and the books I am reading, as well as my daily wanderings through the town, keep this from being wasted time: the impressions flood in upon you even if you do almost nothing. I think I am getting something out of Griswold's *The Religion of the Rigveda*. Young Bajpai is coming to lunch today, and at 5 p.m. I am going to Gandhi's prayer-meeting.

(Later — 6.15 p.m.). The prayer-meeting was genuinely impressive (at this precise point I broke my fountain-pen). I was obliged to be late through no fault of my own. Maria Seville, who was to go with me, was late, and Bob's car was even later. We got to Birla House at 5.20, while the singing of hymns was going on. It doesn't really matter how late one is, actually, as the crowd seems to come and go. All the streets near Birla House are filled with people — the poor, of course, walk for hours to get there.

The prayer-meeting takes place in the garden of Birla House in a sort of summer-house built of red sand stone against the sand stone wall. It looks like this:

Gandhi was seated in a very light-looking wooden chair, portable, in the middle of the summer-house. In front of him on the steps were the women who sing the hymns, the women of his entourage.

Second page. Source: Wisconsin Historical Society, WHI-152590

Appendix 4:
Two Pages from Sheean's Journal,
January 30 and February 6, 1948

On the next pages there are images of the two pages from Sheean's journal dated January 30 and February 6, 1948. He records Mahatma Gandhi's assassination on February 6, ending his January 30 entry before he left to see Gandhi at the prayer meeting. Sheean was present when Gandhi was assassinated on January 30.

Fig. A4.1a: Two pages from Sheean's journal, January 30 and February 6, 1948

He said that "appearances" would do, and for the remainder of the dialogue on this subject we used that word to indicate the physical universe.

His definition of reality is much closer to Ramanuja than to Shankara. He says, of course, that the only living reality is the spirit of God, which is in everything ("including the stones"). Thus all are alive and communicate with one Oversoul. However, this does not mean that physical existence is a dream. It is real in its own sense, as manifestation, although its eventual dissolution is inevitable. (He went off in a long depreciation of scientific knowledge at this point, mostly astronomy, and the point of it apparently was that such sciences give us specific knowledge which is nearly useless, while we neglect the much greater subject of the living reality which is spirit.) —

[I must go now to Ed Snow's dinner for Kingsley Martin — Back to finish this when I can — perhaps not until Friday, as I'm going to Amritsar with Nehru tomorrow.]

Delhi, Friday 30th. Back from Amritsar at 12:45. The trip was a great success for Nehru (of course), as he was greeted by immense crowds everywhere. There were perhaps 150,000 people to hear him at Rambagh Park, where the radio loud speaker refused to work; there were even more this morning at a military review on the parade ground. The schedule was heavy and Nehru around broken with fatigue just from following him around. He made his best speech of the tour in talking to officers of the Indian Army last night, it was in English, which seems to be the officers' language even among themselves — we had dinner: I went to Amritsar clean and go out to Birla House. I thought we were coming back the same day. We (that is Nehru's party) stayed at Circuit House and Colonel Nayar, the young fellow who does the military spokesman job here (a paratrooper, with rows of decorations) took care of me in general, providing me with razor, comb, etc., etc. Ci manccava il toothbrush.

As soon as I can do so, perhaps after I return from the prayer-meeting today, I will write further notes on these conversations with Gandhi (or lessons, rather). I have not had time to get the first one adequately

First page. Source: Wisconsin Historical Society, WHI-152586

Fig. A4.1.b: Two pages from Sheean's journal, January 30 and February 6, 1948

covered yet, and today (if he has time for me) will be already the third.

Friday February 6th — Shortly after writing what precedes this I went to Birla House to the prayer meeting. The Mahatma was a little late and came towards us over the grass, leaning on the girls. I had decided not to talk to him any more about the milk vow, since this obviously pained him somewhat. I was going to go on at once to "The Kingdom of God is Within You", the next one which was the next subject, and then on Saturday I was going to try "Jesus as supreme artist," from the talk he made on art in 1924. On Monday, Feb. 2 he was to have gone to Wardha and I with him. It was my idea to continue these lessons from him in whatever time he had and then to accompany him to the last Punjab or Pakistan, which would have been — according to my feeling of the nature of sacred drama — the last journey: his lesson incomplete in life being completed by death.

However, as he came up the steps of the prayer-ground at about 5:12 or 5:13 — I looked at my watch when he came out of the house and remarked to Bob Stimson, "The Mahatma is late tonight." — some maniac came from the little crowd there and shot him dead. I heard four shots and then seem to have gone into a semi-dazed state for a few moments. I thought his consciousness went then, right away. They say he lived a little longer, but I doubt if the consciousness was there or I would have felt more hope than I did. I didn't go to look (although I was standing four or five yards away) and I didn't see them carry him back to the house and I did not go to look through the glass doors to the room where he lay dying. I wandered in the garden for an hour and a half or thereabouts. Over and again there came texts from the Bible, Shakespeare, etc., flowing through my head. "From the depths I cried to him and he answered me," was one. Another, "Father, why hast thou forsaken me?"

Second page. Source: Wisconsin Historical Society, WHI-152587

Appendix 5:
Sheean's Letter to Ruth Falkenau, a Lifelong Friend, 1927

The letter is reproduced on three pages, starting on this page. In the letter to this lifelong friend, based in Chicago, Sheean mentions the death of Rayna Prohme, his dear friend, who died in Moscow.

Fig. A5.1.a: A three-page letter by Sheean to a lifelong friend, Ruth Falkenau

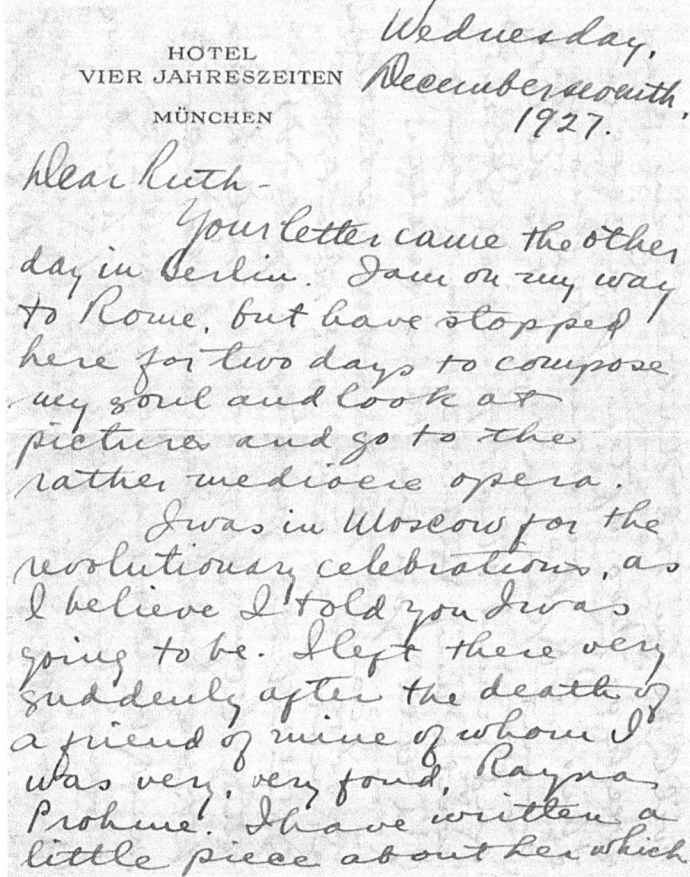

First page. Source: Hanna Holborn Gray Special Collections Research Center, University of Chicago Library

Fig. A5.1.b: A three-page letter by Sheean to a lifelong friend, Ruth Falkenau

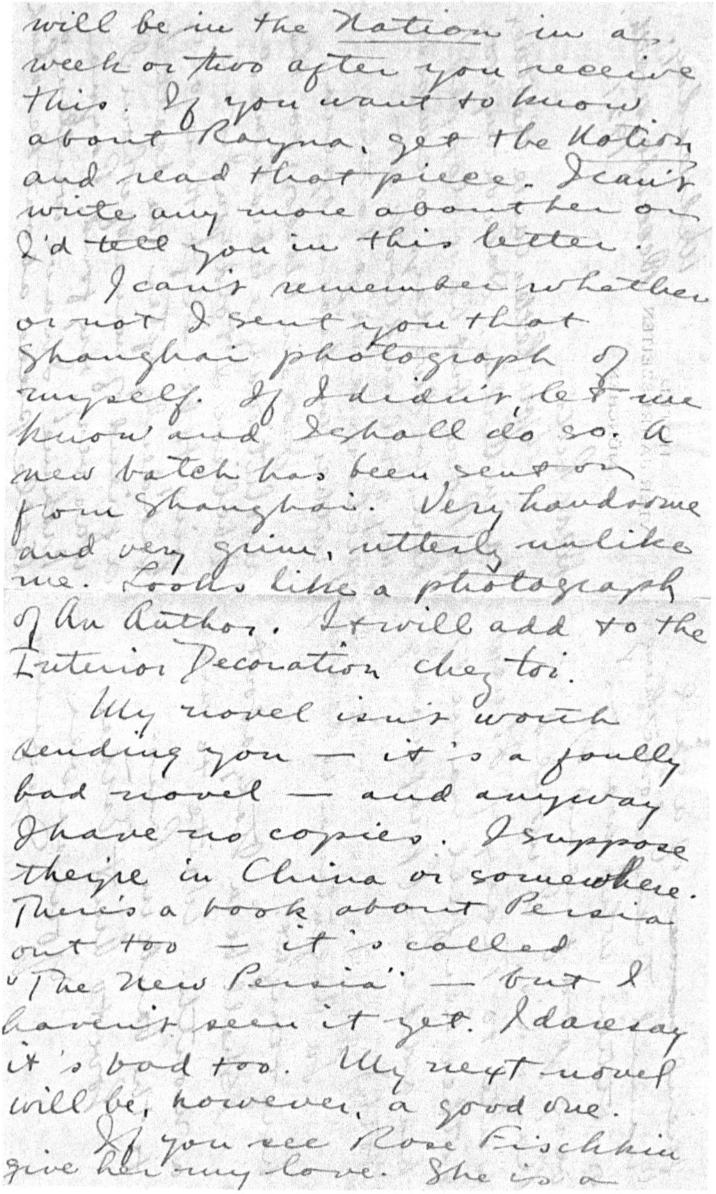

will be in the Nation in a week or two after you receive this. If you want to know about Rayna, get the Nation and read that piece. I can't write any more about her or I'd tell you in this letter.

I can't remember whether or not I sent you that Shanghai photograph of myself. If I didn't let me know and I shall do so. A new batch has been sent on from Shanghai. Very handsome and very grim, utterly unlike me. Looks like a photograph of an Author. It will add to the Interior Decoration chez toi.

My novel isn't worth sending you — it's a foully bad novel — and anyway I have no copies. I suppose they're in China or somewhere. There's a book about Persia out too — it's called "The New Persia" — but I haven't seen it yet. I daresay it's bad too. My next novel will be, however, a good one. If you see Rose Fischkin give her my love. She is a

Second page. Source: Hanna Holborn Gray Special Collections Research Center, University of Chicago Library

Fig. A5.1c: A three-page letter by Sheean to a lifelong friend, Ruth Falkenau

friend ~~names~~ of a girl named Tracy something-or-other who was a very good friend of Raynal's. I would write to Tracy if I knew either her full name or her address (preferably both).

La Argentina is dancing here tonight.

I shall be in Italy about a month. Write to me to the bank in Paris.

Love to Aunt Esther —

Yours ever
Jimmy

Third page. Source: Hanna Holborn Gray Special Collections Research Center, University of Chicago Library

Works Cited

Allard, Elisabeth B. *Spanish National Identity, Colonial Power, and the Portrayal of Muslims and Jews during the Rif War*. Tamesis, 2021.

Alterman, Eric. *We Are Not One: A History of America's Fight over Israel*. Basic Books, 2022.

The Alumni Council of the University of Chicago. "The Blackfriars: 'Barbara, Behave!'" *The University of Chicago Magazine*, XII (7), May 1920, p. 256. The University of Chicago Magazine - Google Books

"Animated, *Adj.*" *Roget's International Thesaurus*, 7th ed., HarperCollins Publishers, 2010, p. 527.

Applegate, Edd. *Literary Journalism: A Biographical Dictionary of Writers and Editors*. Greenwood Press, 1996.

Arlen, Michael J. "Notes on the New Journalism." 1972. *The Reporter as Artist: A Look at the New Journalism Controversy*, edited by Ronald Weber, Communication Arts Books, 1974, pp. 244-254.

"The Art of Reportage." *Lettre Ulysses Award for the Art of Reportage*. Lettre Ulysses Award | The Art of Reportage (lettre-ulysses-award.org)

Bacon, Nora. *The Well-Crafted Sentence: A Writer's Guide to Style*. Bedford/St. Martin's, 2013.

Bak, John S. "Introduction." *Literary journalism across the globe: Journalistic traditions and transnational influences*, edited by John S. Bak and Bill Reynolds, University of Massachusetts Press, 2011, pp. 1-21.

Bak, John S., and Bill Reynolds, editors. *Literary Journalism across the Globe: Journalistic Traditions and Transnational Influences*. University of Massachusetts Press, 2011.

Bak, John S. "Of Troops and Tropes: US Literary War Journalism from the Civil War to the War on Terror." *The Routledge Companion to American Literary Journalism*, edited by William E. Dow and Roberta S. Maguire, Routledge, 2020, pp. 235-255.

Baldick, Chris. *The Oxford Dictionary of Literary Terms*. Oxford University Press, 2015.

Bartel, Roland. *Metaphors and Symbols: Forays into Language*. National Council of Teachers of English, 1983.

Bell, Susan. *The Artful Edit: On the Practice of Editing Yourself*. W. W. Norton & Company, 2007.

Belsey, Catherine. "Textual Analysis as a Research Method." *Research Methods for English Studies*, edited by Gabriele Griffin, 2nd ed., Edinburgh University Press, 2013, pp. 160-178.

Berner, Thomas R. *Writing Literary Features*. Lawrence Erlbaum Associates, 1988.

Bessie, Alvah. *Men in Battle: A Story of Americans in Spain*. Chandler & Sharp Publishers, 1975.

Bordman, Gerald, and Thomas S. Hischak. *The Oxford Companion to American Theatre*. Oxford University Press, 2004. *Google Books*, The Concise Oxford Companion to American Theatre - Gerald Martin Bordman - Google Books

Boynton, Robert S. "Foreword." *The Routledge Companion to American Literary Journalism*, edited by William E. Dow and Roberta S. Maguire, Routledge, 2020, pp. xix-xxi.

Brown, Judith M. *Gandhi: Prisoner of Hope*. Yale University Press, 1989.

Cameron, Meribeth E. Review of *Between the Thunder and the Sun*, by Vincent Sheean. *The Far Eastern Quarterly*, vol. 2, no. 4, August 1943, 379-380. *JSTOR*, https://doi.org/10.2307/2049244.

Canby, Henry S. "The Threatening Thirties: How Books Record the Dominant Emotion of the Current Decade." *The Saturday Review of Literature*, May 22, 1937, pp. 3-4, 14.

Chutchian, Kenneth Z. *John Reed: Radical Journalist, 1887-1920*. McFarland & Company, 2019.

Cohen, Deborah. *Last Call at the Hotel Imperial: The Reporters Who Took on a World at War*. Random House, 2022.

Concise Oxford American dictionary, Oxford University Press, 2006.

Connery, Thomas B. "A Third Way to Tell the Story: American Literary Journalism at the Turn of the Century." *Literary Journalism in the Twentieth Century*, edited by Norman Sims, Oxford University Press, 1990, pp. 3-20.

Connery, Thomas B. "Preface." *A Sourcebook of American Literary Journalism: Representative Writers in an Emerging Genre*, edited by Thomas B. Connery, Greenwood Press, 1992, pp. xii-xiv.

Connery, Thomas B. "Discovering a Literary Form." *A Sourcebook of American Literary Journalism: Representative Writers in an Emerging Genre*, edited by Thomas B. Connery, Greenwood Press, 1992, pp. 3-37.

Connery, Thomas B., editor. *A Sourcebook of American Literary Journalism: Representative Writers in an Emerging Genre*. Greenwood Press, 1992.

Conover, Ted. *Immersion: A Writer's Guide to Going Deep*. The University of Chicago Press, 2016.

Cott, Nancy F. *Fighting Words: The Bold American Journalists Who Brought the World Home between the Wars*. Basic Books, 2020.

Cowley, Malcolm. "The Long View." *The New Republic*, vol. 82, no.1055, 20 February 1935, pp. 50-51. EBSCOhost, https://web.p.ebscohost.com/ehost/detail/detail?vid=9&sid=7886f5a2-a651-412a-8214-898105d0a6bb%40redis&bdata=JnNpdGU9ZWhvc3QtbGl2ZQ%3d%3d#AN=15378053&db=fjh

Daly, Christopher B. *Covering America: A Narrative History of a Nation's Journalism*. University of Massachusetts Press, 2018.

Deighton, Len, and Max Hastings. *Battle of Britain*. Michael Joseph, Penguin Group, 1990.

Denning, Stephen. *The Springboard: How Storytelling Ignites Action in Knowledge-Era Organizations*. Butterworth-Heinemann, 2001.

Dillard, Annie. "Contemporary Prose Styles." *Twentieth Century Literature*, vol. 27, no. 3, 1981, pp. 207–222. https://doi.org/10.2307/441228

Duffus, Robert L. "Mr. Sheean's Post-War Odyssey: His 'Personal History' Is a Thoughtful Record of Adventurous Years." *The New York Times*, 3 February 1935, p. 1, p. 27, TimesMachine: February 3, 1935 - NYTimes.com

Duffus, Robert L. "A New Book by Vincent Sheean: 'Not Peace but a Sword' Stands Above 'Personal History.'" *The New York Times*, 30 July 1939, p. 1, p. 16, TimesMachine: July 30, 1939 - NYTimes.com

Easwaran, Eknath, translator. *The Upanishads*. Nilgiri Press, 2007.

Fenton, Tom. *Bad News: The Decline of Reporting, the Business of News, and the Danger to Us All*. Harper, 2005.

Filloy, Richard. "Orwell's Political Persuasion: A Rhetoric of Personality." *Literary Nonfiction: Theory, Criticism, Pedagogy*, edited by Chris Anderson, Southern Illinois University Press, 1989, pp. 51-69.

Fischer, Louis. "The Boy from Illinois." *The Nation*, vol. 156, no. 16, 17 April 1943, pp. 566-567. The Boy from Illinois: EBSCOhost

Fischer, Louis. "Light from India." *The New York Times*, 17 July 1949, p. 3, p. 24, TimesMachine: July 17, 1949 - NYTimes.com

Fischer, Louis. *The Life of Mahatma Gandhi*. Harper & Row, 1950.

Fischer, Louis. "Highlights and Shadows." *The New York Times*, 24 January 1960, p. 6, p. 28, TimesMachine: January 24, 1960 - NYTimes.com

Flippen, Charles C., editor. *Liberating the Media: The New Journalism*. Acropolis Books, 1974.

Fontaine, Andre, and William A. Glavin, Jr. *The Art of Writing Nonfiction*. Syracuse University Press, 1987.

Gabrial, Brian. "Some Clues to Origins of the Literary Imagination." *Literary Journalism Studies*, vol. 4, no. 1, Spring 2012, p. 142-144.

Georgakopoulou, Alexandra, and Dionysis Goutsos. "Revisiting Discourse Boundaries: The Narrative and Non-Narrative Modes." *Text*, vol. 20, no. 1, 2000, pp. 63-82.

Gornick, Vivian. *The Situation and the Story: The Art of Personal Narrative*. Farrar, Straus and Giroux, 2002.

Gray, James. "The Journalist as Literary Man." *American Non-fiction 1900-1950*, by May Brodbeck, James Gray, and Walter Metzger, Henry Regnery Company, 1952, pp. 95-147.

Haag, Pamela. *Revise: The Scholar-Writer's Essential Guide to Tweaking, Editing, and Perfecting Your Manuscript*. Yale UP, 2021.

Hamilton, John M. *Journalism's Roving Eye: A History of American Foreign Reporting*. Louisiana State UP, 2009.

Hamilton, John M. "Vincent Sheean's *Personal History*." *Second Read: Writers Look Back at Classic Works of Reportage*, edited by James Marcus and the Staff of the Columbia Journalism Review, Columbia University Press, 2012, pp. 124-131.

Harrington, Walt. "Preface: When Writing about Yourself Is Still Journalism." *The Beholder's Eye: A Collection of America's Finest Personal Journalism*, edited by Walt Harrington, 2005, pp. xv-xxii.

Harrington, Walt, and Mike Sager, editors. *Next Wave: America's New Generation of Great Literary Journalists*. The Sager Group, 2012.

Harris, Walter B. *France, Spain and the Rif*. The Naval & Military Press, 2021.

Hart, Jack. *Storycraft: The Complete Guide to Writing Narrative Nonfiction*. The University of Chicago Press, 2021.

Hartsock, John C. *A History of American Literary Journalism: The Emergence of a Modern Narrative Form.* University of Massachusetts Press, 2000.

Hartsock, John C. *Literary Journalism and the Aesthetics of Experience.* University of Massachusetts Press, 2016.

Hartsock, John C. E-mail to the author. 21 December 2022.

Haven, Kendall. *Write Right: Creative Writing Using Storytelling Techniques.* Teacher Ideas Press, 1999.

Hellman, John. *Fables of Fact: The New Journalism as New Fiction.* University of Illinois Press, 1981.

Hersey, John. "Homecoming I-The House on New China Road." *The New Yorker*, 10 May 1982, pp. 49-79.

Hersey, John. "Homecoming II-A Posting to Tientsin." *The New Yorker*, 17 May 1982, pp. 46-70.

Hersey, John. *Hiroshima.* Vintage Books, 2020.

Hesse, Douglas. "Stories in Essays, Essays as Stories." *Literary Nonfiction: Theory, Criticism, Pedagogy*, edited by Chris Anderson, Southern Illinois University Press, 1989, pp. 176-196.

Hertz, Sue. *Write Choices: Elements of Nonfiction Storytelling.* CQ Press, Sage, 2016.

Hirson, Baruch, and Arthur J. Knodel. *Reporting the Chinese Revolution: The Letters of Rayna Prohme*, edited by Gregor Benton, Pluto Press, 2007.

Hoellering, Franz. "Personal History II." *The Nation*, vol. 149, no. 5, 29 July 1939, p. 128. EBSCOhost, Personal History II.: EBSCOhost

Hollowell, John. *Fact & Fiction: The New Journalism and the Nonfiction Novel.* The University of North Carolina Press, 1977.

Hull, Anne. "Being There." *Telling True Stories: A Nonfiction Writers' Guide from the Nieman Foundation at Harvard University*, edited by Mark Kramer and Wendy Call, Plume, Penguin, 2007, pp. 39-45.

Immerwahr, Daniel. "The Books of the Century: 1940-1949." *The Books of the Century.* The Books of the Century, 1940-1949 (berkeley.edu)

Isaacs, Harold R. *The Tragedy of the Chinese Revolution.* Stanford UP, 1961.

"John Hersey." *The New Yorker*, 5 April 1993, p. 111. Apr 05, 1993 (newyorker.com)

Johnson, Carl E. *A Twentieth Century Seeker: A Biography of James Vincent Sheean.* 1974. The University of Wisconsin, PhD thesis. ProQuest Dissertations and Theses A&I.

Jones, Dan R. "John Hersey." *A Sourcebook of American Literary Journalism: Representative Writers in an Emerging Genre*, edited by Thomas B. Connery, Greenwood Press, 1992, pp. 213-221.

Kallan, Richard A. "Tom Wolfe." *A Sourcebook of American Literary Journalism: Representative Writers in an Emerging Genre*, edited by Thomas B. Connery, Greenwood Press, 1992, pp. 249-259.

Keeble, Richard L, and John Tulloch, editors. *Global Literary Journalism: Exploring the Journalistic Imagination*, vol. 2. Peter Lang Publishing, 2014.

Keeble, Richard L. "Introduction." *Global Literary Journalism: Exploring the Journalistic Imagination*, edited by Richard L. Keeble and John Tulloch, vol. 2, Peter Lang Publishing, 2014, pp. 1-16.

Kerrane, Kevin, and Ben Yagoda, editors. *The Art of Fact: A Historical Anthology of Literary Journalism*. Simon & Schuster, 1998.

Kidder, Tracy, and Richard Todd. *Good Prose: The Art of Nonfiction*. Random House, 2013.

Kitchen, Martin. *Europe between the Wars: A Political History*. Longman. 1988.

Kramer, Mark. "Breakable Rules for Literary Journalists." *Literary Journalism: A New Collection of the Best American Nonfiction*, edited by Norman Sims and Mark Kramer, Ballantine Books, 1995, pp. 21-34.

Kramer, Mark. "Coming of Age as a Writer in the Sixties: Realizations about Voice." *The Routledge Companion to American Literary Journalism*, edited by William E. Dow and Roberta S. Maguire, Routledge, 2020, pp. 225-231.

Kramer, Mark, and Wendy Call. "Preface." *Telling True Stories: A Nonfiction Writers' Guide from the Nieman Foundation at Harvard University*, edited by Mark Kramer and Wendy Call, Plume, Penguin Group, 2007, pp. xv-xvii.

Kronenberger, Louis. "European plan." *The New Yorker*, 29 July 1939, pp. 58-59. Jul 29, 1939 (newyorker.com)

Lehman, Daniel W. *Matters of Fact: Reading Nonfiction over the Edge*. Ohio State University Press, 1997.

Lehman, Daniel W. *John Reed & the Writing of Revolution*. Ohio University Press, 2002.

LoBrutto, Vincent. *The Art of Motion Picture Editing: An Essential Guide to Methods, Principles, Processes, and Terminology*. Allworth Press, 2012.

Lounsberry, Barbara. *The Art of Fact: Contemporary Artists of Nonfiction*. Greenwood Press, 1990.

Lounsberry, Barbara. *Writing Creative Nonfiction: The Literature of Reality*, edited by Gay Talese and Barbara Lounsberry, HarperCollins College Publishers, 1996.

Maguire, Miles. "Literary Journalism: Journalism Aspiring to be Literature." *The Routledge Handbook of Magazine Research: The Future of the Magazine Form*, edited by David Abrahamson and Marcia R. Prior-Miller, Routledge, 2015, pp. 362-374.

Maguire, Roberta S., and William E. Dow. "Introduction." *The Routledge Companion to American Literary Journalism*, edited by William E. Dow and Roberta S. Maguire, Routledge, 2020, pp. 1-14.

McCarthy, Mary. "One Man's Road." *The Nation*, vol. 140, no. 3635, 6 March 1935, pp. 282-284. EBSCOhost, One Man's Road.: EBSCOhost

Michaud, Jon. "Eighty-five from the Archive: John Hersey." *The New Yorker*, 8 June 2010. Eighty-Five from the Archive: John Hersey | The New Yorker

Montgomery, Paul L. "Vincent Sheean, Journalist, Dies at 75." *The New York Times*, 17 March 1975, p. 32. TimesMachine: March 17, 1975 - NYTimes.com

Murfin, Ross, and Supryia Ray. *The Bedford Glossary of Critical and Literary Terms*. Bedford/St. Martin's, 2009.

Nanda, Bal R. "Foreword." *An American Witness to India's Partition*, by Phillips Talbot, Sage, 2007, pp. 10-16.

Nayar, Unni. "India and Pakistan." Review of the book "*Lead, Kindly Light*, by Vincent Sheean." *Middle East Journal*, 1949, vol. 3, no. 4, 475-476.

Nelson, Cary, and Jefferson Hendricks, editors. *Madrid 1937: Letters of the Abraham Lincoln Brigade from the Spanish Civil War*. Routledge, 2013.

Orwell, George. *A Collection of Essays*. Harvest. Harcourt, 1981.

Parratt, Sonia. "Literary Journalism in Spain: Past, Present, (and Future?)." *Literary journalism across the globe: Journalistic traditions and transnational influences*, edited by John S. Bak and Bill Reynolds, University of Massachusetts Press, 2011, pp. 134-147.

Percy, Walker. *Signposts in a Strange Land*. Farrar, Straus and Giroux, 1991.

Poore, Charles. "Books of the Times." *The New York Times*, L 15, 28 July 1939, TimesMachine: July 28, 1939 - NYTimes.com

Rajan, Nalini. "Indian Literary Journalism in the Age of Mobile Phones." *Global Literary Journalism: Exploring the Journalistic Imagination*, edited by Richard L. Keeble and John Tulloch, vol. 2, Peter Lang Publishing, 2014, pp. 261-276.

Reed, John. *Ten Days That Shook the World*. Penguin Books. 1977.

Rees Cheney, Theodore. A. *Writing Creative Nonfiction: How to Use Fiction Techniques to Make Your Nonfiction More Interesting, Dramatic—and Vivid*. Writer's Digest Books, 1987.

Review of *Between the Thunder and the Sun*, by Vincent Sheean. "The Atlantic Bookshelf." The Atlantic, May 1943, Between the Thunder and the Sun – The Atlantic

Roberts, Nancy L. "Literary Journalism and Social Activism." *The Routledge Companion to American Literary Journalism*, edited by William E. Dow and Roberta S. Maguire, Routledge, 2020, pp. 256-268.

Rosenstone, Robert A. *Romantic Revolutionary: A Biography of John Reed*. Vintage Books, 1981.

Ryan, Marie-Laure. "Narrative." *Routledge Encyclopedia of Narrative Theory*, edited by David Herman, Manfred Jahn, and Marie-Laure Ryan, Routledge, 2008, pp. 344-348.

Schudson, Michael. *Discovering the News: A Social History of American Newspapers*. Basic Books, 1978.

Scranton, Roy. "How John Hersey Bore Witness." *The New Republic*, 27 June 2019. How John Hersey Bore Witness | The New Republic

Sheean, Vincent. "16 Die in Ruhr Riots; Hungry Mobs Pillage: Plea of Starving for Food Scorned." *Chicago Tribune*, 26 November 1923, pp. 1-32. https://www.newspapers.com, 26 Nov 1923, 1 - Chicago Tribune at Newspapers.com

Sheean, Vincent. *Personal History*. The Literary Guild, 1935.

Sheean, Vincent. *Not Peace but a Sword*. Doubleday, Doran & Company, 1939.

Sheean, Vincent. *Between the Thunder and the Sun*. Random House, 1943.

Sheean, Vincent. *This House against This House*. Random House, 1945.

Sheean, Vincent. "Present Day American Tragedy." *Nieman Reports*, vol. 1, no.2, April 1947, pp. 16-17. Retrieved from Nieman Reports

Sheean, Vincent. *Lead, Kindly Light*. Random House, 1949.

Sheean, Vincent. *Nehru: The Years of Power*. Random House, 1960.

Shenker, Israel. "Vincent Sheean at 75 Ponders His and the World's State." *The New York Times*, 6 December 1974, p. 41, p. 53. TimesMachine: December 6, 1974 - NYTimes.com

Sims, Norman. "The Literary Journalists." *The Literary Journalists*, edited by Norman Sims, Ballantine Books, 1984, pp. 3-25.

Sims, Norman. "Preface." *Literary Journalism in the Twentieth Century*, edited by Norman Sims, Oxford University Press, 1990, pp. v-x.

Sims, Norman. "The Art of Literary Journalism." *Literary Journalism: A New Collection of the Best American Nonfiction*, edited by Norman Sims and Mark Kramer, Ballantine Books, 1995, pp.3-20.

Sims, Norman, and Mark Kramer, editors. *Literary Journalism: A New Collection of the Best American Nonfiction*. Ballantine Books, 1995.

Sims, Norman. *True Stories: A Century of Literary Journalism*. Northwestern University Press, 2007.

Snow, Edgar. *Journey to the Beginning*. Vintage Books, 1972.

Snyder, Louis L., and Richard B. Morris, editors. *A Treasury of Great Reporting: "Literature under Pressure" from the Sixteenth Century to Our Own Time*. Simon and Schuster, 1962.

Sood, Raj. "Marine Endures War in POW Camp." Liberation – *Guam Remembers: A Golden Salute for the 50th Anniversary of the Liberation of Guam*, edited by Tony Palomo and Paul J. Borja, 1994. War in the Pacific NHP: Liberation - Guam Remembers (nps.gov)

Stanzel, Franz K. *A Theory of Narrative*. Translated by Charlotte Goedsche, Cambridge University Press, 1986.

Stewart, Kenneth. *News Is What We Make It: A Running Story of the Working Press*. Houghton Mifflin Company. The Riverside Press, 1943.

Strang, Lewis C. *Famous Actresses of the Day in America*. Boston: L. C. Page and Company, 1902. #13 - Famous actresses of the day in America. - Full View | HathiTrust Digital Library

Talbot, Phillips. *An American Witness to India's Partition*. Sage, 2007.

Talese, Gay, and Barbara Lounsberry, editors. *Writing Creative Nonfiction: The Literature of Reality*. HarperCollins College Publishers, 1996.

Taylor, Alan J. P. "Introduction." *Ten Days That Shook the World*, by John Reed, Penguin Books, 1977, (pp. vii-xix).

Thompson, Craig. "Mr. Sheean's Prelude to War." *The New York Times*, 28 March 1943, p. 4. https://timesmachine.nytimes.com/timesmachine/1943/03/28/83911650.pdf?pdf_redirect=true&ip=0

Treglown, Jeremy. *Mr. Straight Arrow: The Career of John Hersey, Author of Hiroshima*. Farrar, Straus and Giroux, 2019.

Underwood, Doug. "Literary Journalism and American Magazines." *The Routledge Companion to American Literary Journalism*, edited by William E. Dow and Roberta S. Maguire, Routledge, 2020, pp. 269-287.

Warnock, John. "Introduction." *Representing Reality: Readings in Literary Nonfiction*, edited by John Warnock, St. Martin's Press, 1989, pp. xvii-xx.

Weber, Ronald. *The Literature of Fact: Literary Nonfiction in American Writing*. Ohio University Press, 1980.

Weber, Ronald. *News of Paris: American Journalists in the City of Light between the Wars*. Ivan R. Dee, 2006.

Williams, Albert R. *Journey into Revolution: Petrograd, 1917-1918.* Quadrangle Books, 1969.

Williams, Jospeh M., and Joseph Bizup. *Style: Lessons in Clarity and Grace.* Pearson, 2014.

Wilson, Christopher P. "Chapter 1: Introduction and First Principles." *Reading Narrative Journalism,* 2020. Reading Narrative Journalism (2020) (bc.edu). International Association for Literary Journalism Studies. Resources & Links. https://ialjs.org/ialjs-links/

Wilson, Edmund. *The Shores of Light: A Literary Chronicle of the Twenties and Thirties.* Farrar, Straus and Young, 1952.

Winder, Alex. "The 'Western Wall' Riots of 1929: Religious Boundaries and Communal Violence." *Journal of Palestine Studies,* vol. 42, no. 1, 2012, pp. 6-23.

Wolfe, Tom. *The New Journalism: With an Anthology edited by Tom Wolfe and Edward W. Johnson.* Harper & Row, 1973.

Woolbert, Robert G. "Capsule Review of *Between the Thunder and the Sun* by Vincent Sheean." *Foreign Affairs,* October 1943. Between the Thunder and the Sun | Foreign Affairs

Yagoda, Ben. "Preface." *The Art of Fact: A Historical Anthology of Literary Journalism,* edited by Kevin Kerrane and Ben Yagoda, Simon & Schuster, 1998, pp. 13-16.

Young, Stanley. "Jessie Was a Lady." The New York Times, 3 May 1964, p. 6, p. 40. https://timesmachine.nytimes.com/timesmachine/1964/05/03/118659348.html?pageNumber=174

Zdovc, Sonja M. "Željko Kozinc, The Subversive Reporter: Literary Journalism in Slovenia." *Literary Journalism across the Globe: Journalistic Traditions and Transnational Influences,* edited by John S. Bak, and Bill Reynolds, University of Massachusetts Press, 2011, pp. 238-259.

Zettl, Herbert. *Sight, Sound, Motion: Applied Media Aesthetics,* 4th ed. Thomson Wadsworth, 2005.

Zipp, Samuel. *The Idealist: Wendell Willkie's Wartime Quest to Build One World.* The Belknap Press, Harvard University Press, 2020.

Index

A

action, 3, 4, 13, 18, 22, 41, 42, 43, 44, 45, 46, 48, 49, 50, 52, 53, 67, 69, 75, 128

B

Between the Thunder and the Sun, 9, 30, 33, 77, 78, 79, 80, 81, 86, 103, 104, 134
Britain, 77, 79, 82, 128

C

characters, 3, 5, 16, 42, 43, 44, 45, 50, 56, 60, 62, 65, 69, 71, 73, 75, 80, 86, 88, 91, 98, 103
China, 20, 30, 36, 37, 38, 39, 43, 51, 55, 56, 77, 82, 100, 130
chronological structure, 23
close reading, 9, 10, 11
coherence, 23, 24, 55
cohesion, 32, 41, 42, 43, 44, 54, 56, 57
concrete details, 3, 4, 23, 25, 75, 79

D

definitions, 2
discursive, 5, 59, 60, 76, 98
discursive literary journalism, 59

E

el-Krim, Abd, 38, 45, 46, 47, 49, 50
exhaustive research, 4, 38
exposition, 5, 16, 22, 23, 24, 25, 26, 40, 42, 45, 46, 48, 49, 52, 59, 72, 80, 86, 87

F

fiction, 1, 2, 4, 5, 8, 13, 20, 29, 43, 47, 129, 130, 132
fine writing, 4, 23, 61, 75
foreign reporters or correspondents, 1
form, 1, 2, 3, 4, 5, 6, 7, 10, 12, 18, 23, 25, 26, 27, 36, 37, 40, 43, 54, 57, 59, 61, 66, 67, 76, 77, 92, 97, 108, 128, 130, 131
France, 30, 46, 47, 59, 77, 79, 80, 82, 84, 85

G

Gandhi, Mahatma, 31, 32, 33, 87, 88, 89, 90, 91, 92, 93, 95, 97, 99, 101, 128
genre, 1, 2, 3, 4, 5, 6, 7, 9, 10, 21, 30, 61, 128, 130

H

Hersey, John, 4, 9, 11, 12, 20, 21, 27, 130, 131, 132, 133

Hiroshima, 4, 9, 12, 13, 20, 21, 22, 23, 24, 25, 26, 27, 130, 133
historical narrative, 3, 40, 46, 48

I

imagery & symbolism, 4, 23
immersion, 3, 6, 19, 79, 87, 88, 91, 92, 97, 102, 103
India, 31, 33, 87, 88, 89, 91, 92, 94, 97, 98, 99, 100, 101, 102, 129, 131, 133
International Brigades, 62

J

Jimmy. See *Sheean, Vincent*

L

Lardner, Jim, 62
Lead, Kindly Light, 9, 31, 32, 33, 87, 88, 94, 95, 97, 103, 104, 131
Lettre Ulysses Award for the Art of Reportage, 2
Lincoln Battalion, 62
Literary journalism, 1, 86, 97
literary nonfiction, 10
literary reportage, 5
literature, 1, 4, 5, 12, 23, 28, 42, 61, 94, 131, 133

M

Morocco, 29, 35, 39, 43, 45, 46, 49
muckraking, 7

N

narrative and rhetorical techniques, 2
narrative literary journalism, 5, 7, 8, 10
narrative yellow or sensational journalism, 7
narratives, 3, 5, 33, 40, 41, 42, 44, 50, 51, 56, 60, 62, 76, 98
National Book Award, 28, 35
Nehru, Jawaharlal, 31, 33, 89, 97, 98, 101
Nehru: The Years of Power, 9
New Journalism, 3, 5, 8, 10, 21, 27
new reportage, 5
nonfiction, 2, 4, 5, 6, 8, 9, 10, 21, 41, 42, 43, 98, 103, 104, 129, 130, 131, 132, 133
Not Peace but a Sword, 9, 30, 33, 59, 60, 61, 74, 75, 76, 77, 86, 103, 104, 129

P

Pana, Illinois, 28
Personal History, 9, 27, 30, 32, 35, 36, 38, 39, 40, 41, 42, 43, 44, 50, 54, 55, 56, 57, 59, 60, 61, 74, 75, 76, 77, 86, 87, 94, 103, 104, 128, 129, 130
premonition, 31, 87, 95
presence, 33, 42, 44, 56
Prohme, Rayna, 35, 36, 44, 51, 52, 53, 54, 63, 75

R

Reed, John, 8, 9, 11, 12, 13, 14, 15, 18, 20, 27, 128, 131, 132
reportage, 5, 6, 8, 129
Rif, 29, 35, 37, 38, 39, 43, 44, 45, 46, 47, 48, 49, 50, 51, 55, 80

Index 137

Russia, 14, 16, 19, 20, 30, 35, 39, 43, 51, 55, 77, 82, 100

S

saturation reporting, 29
scene, 3, 4, 10, 14, 18, 21, 22, 30, 40, 41, 42, 49, 69, 71, 72, 73, 74, 75, 84, 98
Sheean, Vincent, 2, 9, 12, 27, 28, 29, 30, 31, 32, 35, 36, 37, 38, 39, 40, 43, 44, 45, 46, 47, 48, 49, 50, 51, 52, 53, 54, 55, 56, 57, 59, 60, 61, 62, 63, 64, 65, 66, 67, 68, 69, 70, 71, 72, 73, 74, 75, 76, 77, 78, 79, 80, 81, 82, 83, 85, 86, 87, 88, 89, 90, 91, 92, 93, 94, 95, 97, 98, 99, 100, 101, 102, 103, 108, 128, 129, 130, 131, 132, 133, 134
  Jimmy:, 28
Spain, 1, 6, 9, 29, 30, 43, 45, 46, 47, 59, 61, 64, 65, 69, 71, 72, 75, 79, 82, 127, 132
Spanish republic, 62, 69, 75, 76, 79, 82
status details, 61
Stories, 1, 3, 5, 41, 43, 130

story, 2, 3, 5, 7, 15, 16, 20, 21, 24, 29, 31, 33, 37, 40, 41, 43, 44, 45, 47, 49, 50, 51, 52, 54, 55, 59, 61, 62, 64, 66, 67, 69, 71, 78, 87, 88, 91, 92, 99, 127, 128, 129, 133
Story Structure, 46, 52
structure, 3, 16, 23, 24, 33, 40, 41, 42, 43, 45, 46, 47, 52, 78, 92
subjective, 19, 33, 80, 85, 86, 94
summary, 12, 22, 40, 91
symbol, 83, 93, 97, 98, 99
symbolic realities, 3

T

Ten Days That Shook the World, 9, 12, 13, 14, 15, 27
textual analysis, 9

W

world, 2, 4, 5, 6, 13, 19, 25, 27, 28, 30, 35, 36, 37, 41, 50, 56, 59, 60, 69, 71, 74, 75, 77, 79, 83, 85, 86, 87, 88, 89, 91, 94, 103, 104, 128, 132, 133, 134

www.ingramcontent.com/pod-product-compliance
Lightning Source LLC
Chambersburg PA
CBHW070737230426
43669CB00014B/2484